YOUR MOTHER WAS RIGHT

YOUR MOTHER WAS RIGHT

15 Unexpected Lessons About Leadership and the Brain

SANDRA MCDOWELL

Your Mother Was Right: 15 Unexpected Lessons About Leadership and the Brain

For further information about online leadership and coaching training, webinars, speaking and workshops, visit:

SandraMcDowell.com
e-LeadershipAcademy.com

ISBN: 978-1-7750404-0-8

Printed in Canada

Editor: Chantel Hamilton
Style/Copy Editor: Sheila Cameron
Copywriter: Ryan Parton
Designer: Jessica Thomson
Proofreader: Kyla Lane

*To the two remarkable sons
who call me Mom,*

*and the incredible woman
I call Mom.*

CONTENTS

ACKNOWLEDGMENTS

Writing this book has been unlike any other undertaking that I have put my mind to. Without the encouragement of my husband, Matt, and sons, Austin and Carter, I would never have been able to make it happen. I thank them for their patience and for always being my biggest cheerleaders.

I'm grateful for the expertise and guidance of the professionals who helped me complete this book, especially my lifelong friend, Sheila Cameron, whose unwavering support and literary prowess got me to the finish line.

Much appreciation goes to Dave Craigen for empowering me to reach this milestone by supporting my passion for learning and leadership. Special thanks to Charlene Reinisch for being a sounding board for my ideas and encouraging me in the moments when I needed it most.

And most importantly, I wish to extend tremendous gratitude and love to my mom, Elaine, and father, George, for their unconditional love and guidance and for all the lessons that are now woven into the fabric of my being when leading myself and others.

FOREWORD

For more than twenty years, I have watched Sandra McDowell exceed the expectations of those around her with every endeavour. Again and again, it seems she does things that were unimaginable in the previous year. From her executive role, to speaking on international stages, to leadership awards, to her impressive online leadership program, her accomplishments have appeared ceaseless. Yet, not a single one of them has come as a surprise to me.

Sandra is always moving forward. Her ongoing success is a direct result of a tremendous work ethic. It is this quality that I find most inspirational, and I believe it is also the reason that people have so much to learn from her. Her appetite for learning has enabled her to acquire a wealth of experience and knowledge on the subjects of leadership, coaching, and brain health.

This book represents a culmination of her knowledge about leadership and the brain, along with her passion to help people lead themselves and others more effectively. The book uses timeless lessons shared by mothers to illustrate the simplicity of their wisdom—we all have things that we learned from our mothers.

When I was younger, I had a tendency to speak first and listen later. I was confident in my intelligence and opinions. In some respects, this confidence was a good quality, but it wasn't always helpful. My mother noticed this problem, and she explained how changing my attitude would change my relationships.

It was simple. If I hacked a couple notches off my ego and allowed others' opinions a chance to sit in my mind before discounting them, I could learn from them. And at the same time, I would be strengthening relationships by offering my attention. Today, my ability to listen and be understanding is one of my favourite parts of who I am, and I'm grateful for my mother's guidance in this regard. After reading this book—where I learned more about threat responses and the social brain—I now understand why this change of attitude made such a difference when interacting with others.

Like the lessons offered in this book, my mother's advice was simple—and it helped me dramatically. I just needed a nudge and the facts to support why making the effort would help me. And that is exactly what the reader has to gain within these pages: elementary lessons with scientific evidence to give them weight. After examining each one of them, you might even come to the unnerving conclusion that *your* mother was right!

It is my honour to invite you, the reader, to enjoy the writings of Sandra Mc-Dowell—an incredible woman who is a model for leadership and supporting the growth of others. A woman I appreciate more and more as I've come to realize that each lesson she's shown me has some deeper significance. A woman who taught me to read, to eat my greens, and how to fold my shirts. A woman I am privileged to call my mother.

Austin Phillips

INTRODUCTION

When I told my mom the title of the leadership book I was writing, she reacted exactly as one might expect. "So I was right?" she said. Validation was evident in her voice. She even called back a few hours later to confirm the book's title before calling my aunt to tell *her* about it. And who can fault my mom for her pride? After raising six strong-willed children, she finally had affirmation for all the times she thought or gently implied, "I told you so."

As it turns out, my studies of neuroscience and leadership *had* revealed to me a surprising truth: all mothers—and parents in general—have been right all along with their advice to help us think more clearly and effectively. The maxims they've been asserting for years—like "Go to bed!" and "Use your words!"—reflect scientifically proven truths about what is good for the brain, leadership, and the overall health of our species.

While our mothers may not have understood the neuroscience that made their statements true, they almost certainly felt compelled to share their inherent wisdom with us. If you have children, you may have passed on the same comments yourself: "You are what you eat," "Count to 10," "It's not the end of the world." These maxims persist because, at a fundamental level, we all know they're true.

So, what's the relation between Mom's advice and leadership in the workplace?

Change, and especially organizational change, is one of the most difficult aspects of leadership. As an executive coach, I've worked with many people who, despite wanting to change, didn't know where to start. If they did make modest progress toward their goals, they often returned to their old habits after a short while. As an executive at a financial institution for the last 15 years, I have witnessed first-hand how good intentions—both personal and organizational—have been squelched by people falling back to their old ways of doings things.

Through continued studies of neuroscience, I now have a much deeper understanding of what gets in between those good intentions and reality, and I've learned how to work with the brain to lead myself and others more effectively.

I've worked diligently to help build leadership and coaching capabilities both collectively and individually, and I've discovered that—for the most part—the solution to affecting real lasting change is easy enough to comprehend. But the missing link is a better understanding of the brain—and a willingness to embrace the lessons we learned in our earliest years.

A neurological approach to leadership looks at actual brain science and shows how a well-conditioned brain can be a catalyst for high-performance leadership. Neuroscience, as it relates to leadership, is a vital topic that has been underexplored, at least at a level that's understandable and relatable for professionals looking to grow their leadership knowledge and effectiveness. And what could be more relatable than our own mothers? The easiest and most understandable way to share these powerful brain truths is to bring it all back to the most relevant and memorable lessons from Mom.

Based on the burgeoning field of study known as neuroleadership, this book will reinforce the things you (and Mom) already know, while simultaneously confirming these truths from the perspective of brain science. An understanding of neuroleadership empowers us to apply the learnings from the field of neuroscience to the practice of personal and organizational leadership.

I offer hands-on executive leadership experience—including time spent in the roles of interim CEO and COO—along with a Master of Arts in leadership, a certified executive coach (PCC) designation, and a certificate in neuroleadership, but I am not a neuroscientist. When it comes to the brain, I rely on the brilliant work of today's leading neuroscientists—those who are in the field researching and conducting studies that are shedding more light on the science and psychology behind how our minds and bodies work.

It's been said that ignorance is bliss. While that may be true to some extent, its opposite—knowledge is power—is even truer for today's leaders. Floating along in a bubble of oblivion may be more comfortable, but the lessons within this book will divulge how and why this may not be working for you, and those you lead, in terms of being able to think and perform.

This book will help you see the strong connection between neuroscience, leadership, common sense advice, and the workplace. It will meet you in that intersection, where neuroscience is playing out in real life and with real possibility and consequence. Perhaps most importantly, this book will reveal the hidden forces that push back against you and those you lead, hijack productivity, and result in sub-par engagement and performance. My goal is to show how you and others are being influenced at a subconscious level, and then point out strategies—based on Mom's advice—to create a better working environment for yourself and those you lead.

Explained through a series of age-old and unexpected "lessons" from Mom, you'll learn how the brain is working against you and others, and how to:

PART II - fuel the brain in terms of sleep, nutrition and activity;

PART III - minimize perceived threats that can cause stress and get in the way of thinking and performance for yourself and others;

PART IV - harness the power of the "social brain" for better teamwork and collaboration;

PART V - create workplace conditions that foster focus, which will increase memory, insight, accuracy and overall well-being for yourself and others; and

PART VI - help yourself and others carve new neuropathways in the brain in order to facilitate better thinking and sustainable change.

But before we explore all the things our mothers used to say that were more accurate than even they probably realized, let's take a bird's-eye view of the workplace in Part I to see why it's more important than ever that we start following Mom's advice.

PART I

THE PROBLEM & THE SOLUTION

PROBLEM: AN EPIDEMIC OF DISENGAGEMENT

Many leaders are not connecting effectively with those they lead, and disconnection is costing organizations both time and money. Common leadership practices either aren't working to the extent they could be or simply aren't working at all.

A recent Gallup study showed that the majority of North American employees (54%) are "not engaged," meaning they are less likely to put effort toward achieving organizational goals. A further 18% are "actively disengaged," meaning they're actually sabotaging the efforts of the rest of the team, are toxic to the work environment and likely spreading their toxicity to others. This adds up to a whopping 72% of employees who are either not contributing to their organization or are actively working against it![1] This isn't just an issue in North America, though. The same Gallup study found that only 13% of employees worldwide are actively engaged at work.

Research conducted by the Deloitte Center for the Edge revealed that as many as 88% of workers aren't passionate about their work and, as a result, they don't contribute to their full potential. The report showed slightly higher levels of "passion" among senior management, although the fact that only around 20% of senior management claims to be passionate about what they do still suggests a larger problem.[2]

As you read this section of the book, consider the research through two lenses. First, through the lens of your organization. What's going on within your organization that may be contributing to disengagement? Second, consider it through the lens of self. How engaged are you as a leader? What's working for you, and what's not working? If you're fortunate, you work in a place where overall engagement is above average. I'm grateful that I've worked in a place where engagement scores are over 80%. But that still means that nearly 20% of people aren't engaged in the vision and goals of the organization. There is so much focus on decreasing costs and increasing revenue, but what about the untapped human capital that we're already spending money on? With 80% engagement, there is 20% opportunity to tap into the discretionary effort of those not yet engaged.

From an organizational perspective, disengaged team members are more likely to call in sick, waste management's time, negatively influence coworkers, and even drive customers away. Like a virus of discontent, disengaged employees work against organizational goals, either actively or passively undoing the great work done by others who are highly engaged and motivated to help their organizations succeed.

Stress, Disengagement and the Financial Impact

While organizations work at warding off external threats such as competitors or market fluctuations, a large portion of their supposed team members have been sabotaging their efforts and slowly eating away at the organization from the inside out. Disengagement—especially active disengagement—undoubtedly affects morale, team dynamics and organizational capacity. It also, unsurprisingly, carries a financial price tag. Studies have shown that more than $350 billion is lost in North America every year because of disengaged employees.[3]

Disengagement is much more than someone not liking their job or not giving discretionary effort. From a personal perspective, health issues among disengaged employees are a major concern. According to research done by Gallup, "The workplace can be linked to serious physical and mental illnesses such as clinical depression and chronic anxiety that can have a significant negative impact on workers' job performance and on their personal lives."[4] When employees aren't physically or mentally well at work because of stress and poor self-care, this impacts the bottom line. In addition to lost productivity, there are increased costs of employee benefits such as short- and long-term leave, prescription drugs, employee and family counseling premiums, and extended benefits such as massage and acupuncture.

Workplaces are stressed to a degree never before seen in history. One study by Towers Watson of 22,347 employees across 12 countries found that "employees suffering from high stress levels have lower engagement, are less productive, and have higher absentee levels than those not operating under excessive pressure."[5] Another study reported that only 8% of Americans report low levels of stress![6] These high levels of stress—while dangerous in their own right—contribute to other epidemics of poor nutrition, sedentary lifestyles and sleeplessness, all of which we'll explore in greater detail in Part II.

Who's to Blame for Disengagement?

A better question might be: who is responsible for engagement—the leader or those they lead? Like everything important, this isn't a black or white issue. Organizations need to ensure they have leaders in place who can articulate the vision or goals, connect with those they lead, and create a culture that is conducive to thinking, trust, collaboration and performance. And as individuals, we need to take personal responsibility to make sure we're working in a place that aligns with our values, and we need to take care of ourselves so that we can show up at work with the ability to think, connect with others, focus and perform.

The responsibility lies with each party. This is why self-awareness is the cornerstone of personal and organizational leadership. Through noticing our habits, assumptions and patterns, we can assess what is working and what is not working in terms of our effectiveness. As leaders, we need to be self-aware and take responsibility for our own well-being and engagement. With a handle on that, we then need to help those we lead increase their self-awareness and accountability for focus, relatedness and performance.

Generally speaking, organizations and employees share the common goal of wanting to make a difference for their customers and communities in which they live. When we look at the research and see that we've gone down a path of stress and disengagement, we can't help but feel a sense of urgency to find new approaches to leading others. So, what can we do differently? How can we change the epidemic of disengagement and the course of our organizations' futures?

We need a new kind of leadership, a leadership that's rooted in an understanding of how our actions—and inactions—affect our performance and the performance of the people around us. Today, we must lead ourselves and others differently than we have for the last few decades—with the knowledge of brain science to support us in a new style of leadership.

SOLUTION: LEADING WITH THE BRAIN IN MIND

In my work with leaders around the world, I talk about "leading with the brain in mind," which essentially means combining basic neuroscience with the principles of leadership for leading self and others.

Like all effective leadership, leading with the brain in mind starts with personal leadership. Often, people find themselves in leadership positions without first mastering the ability to lead themselves; only once you know how to lead yourself can you successfully lead others. It all starts with the Latin concept of nosce te ipsum—"Know thyself." Though it's often uncomfortable to turn the lens inward, any insight into your weaknesses, imbalances and "growth opportunities" (as I like to call them) will ultimately strengthen your leadership impact.

As the Cheshire Cat famously said to Alice, "If you don't know where you're going, then any road will take you there." The road to effective leadership begins with a clear vision of what matters most to you or your organization, and an understanding of what it will take to achieve the goals at hand. The concept of self-awareness has been a common leadership thread throughout history.

Of course, the formula isn't quite as simple as "know thyself and know success." It's one thing to recognize what's not working for your personal or organizational leadership and quite another to do something about it. Through a better understanding of the brain—our own and that of those we work with and lead—we can work with it rather than against it.

Understanding the brain, and analyzing neuroscience and engagement research, has given me much insight into the forces working for and against personal and organizational engagement in the workplace. I've been responsible for overseeing the collection and analysis of employee engagement data for twenty years and have found several things to be constant. First, great leaders have highly-engaged employees. Second, good leaders are good for business, and bad leaders are bad for business. And finally, there is a necessary interplay between an organization's responsibility to create conditions for engaged employees, and a personal responsibility to take care of ourselves and create conditions for high personal engagement.

Everyone is responsible for employee engagement within an organization, from the most senior position to the most junior, and every individual plays a central role in his or her own personal engagement. How we take care of ourselves, how we manage ourselves when feeling threatened, how we relate to others, how we focus, and how we respond to change—all these factors affect our own personal well-being and engagement.

The return on investment of engagement is significant. An Aon Hewitt report noted that a 5% increase in employee engagement correlates with a 3% increase in revenue growth the subsequent year. The report also indicated that "positivity, industriousness, achievement orientation, enthusiasm, cooperation, and sensitivity are predictive of whether a leader will be engaged and engaging of others."[7] Keep those attributes in mind as you read this book.

The Brain

Let's take a quick look at an organ we think about far too infrequently: the brain. Our mothers often told us, "Use your head," but what does that actually mean?

The fundamental goal of our brain is to keep us alive by maximizing rewards (like food, money, and friendship), and minimizing threats (like physical harm, sickness, or being excluded). This should be relatively easy to do in developed parts of the world where we have ample access to natural resources, education, healthcare, and each other. Unfortunately, it's easier said than done.

Although our ability to think is highly evolved and has allowed us to accomplish some pretty phenomenal things, it is affected by a lot more than we realize. Our minds, and the minds of those we lead, are operating against great odds. For the sake of simplicity, I'm going to discuss these odds in the context of two parts: the "emotional brain" and the "thinking brain."

Your emotional brain, technically known as the limbic system, adds emotional context to all that you see, hear, smell, taste and touch. Understanding what can trigger or overtax your emotional brain—and learning strategies to regulate these triggers—is critically important both in terms of individual happiness and your ability to lead others. Your amygdala, which resides in your limbic system, is essential for feeling emotions and perceiving the emotions of others—you actually have two amygdalae, but most commonly, and for the purpose of this book, it is referred to singularly as amygdala. The amygdala is also vital for regulating emotions, but it doesn't always work with us in the way we want it to. It often causes additional problems, especially when we are not taking care of our overall brain health. We'll look further at the amygdala and our fight-or-flight response in Part III.

The thinking brain, more technically known as the cortex or more specifically, the prefrontal cortex (PFC), is the largest, most developed region of the brain. This is where all of your conscious and high-level thought takes place. It's where you analyze information, recognize patterns, create strategies, store memories and solve problems. Think of the PFC as being like an orchestra conductor. It serves to orchestrate the thinking you need to do on a day-to-day basis. The thinking brain can override the sometimes-irrational emotional brain, but its ability to do so is based on a person's cognitive control abilities. This is otherwise known as emotional regulation—a concept we'll also explore in greater detail in Part III.

The Brain and Leadership

Gone is the industrial age, when we got paid for performing manual labour. Today, we live in the age of information. We get paid to think, and our ability to do just that is our biggest value proposition as leaders.

The concept of "know thyself" is particularly important when it comes to understanding how your brain works, how it processes information, how it reacts under threat and in social situations, and perhaps most importantly, the shortcuts it wants to take (to minimize energy expenditure) when facing change. As a leader, however, not only do you have to understand your own brain for effective performance and well-being, but you have the added responsibility of optimizing conditions for problem-solving, decision-making, creativity, and collaboration for all those around you.

Neuroscience gives us evidence as to why we behave the way we do, and although neuroscience isn't new, its application to leadership and organizational behaviour is. Neuroscience leads to insight on how to work within our biological parameters to lead ourselves and others most effectively. The essence of the study of neuroleadership is to understand what is going on inside the minds of those you lead so that you can create conditions that foster better performance and higher levels of engagement.

Great news! It turns out that you already know this stuff. Many of the lessons within this book are things you've learned before. You'll surely recognize most—if not all—of the lessons from your own childhood, such as when your mother told you to "Pay attention!" or "Count to 10." These lessons are just as important for your leadership role and goals today as they were when you were growing up.

In other words, your mother was right.

Somewhere along the way, however—perhaps long ago as a child, or perhaps more recently as an adult—you may have decided that your mother's so-called words of wisdom don't apply to you. After all, you're an adult now. You can make your own rules, right?

Science tells us this just isn't the case. Nobody is above Mom's simple truths because they directly relate to our innate physiology and psychology. Accepting these truths and learning how to work with them—rather than against them—will dramatically improve well-being and engagement for yourself and those you lead.

Now let's jump into the neuroscience behind all those lessons our mothers shared with us.

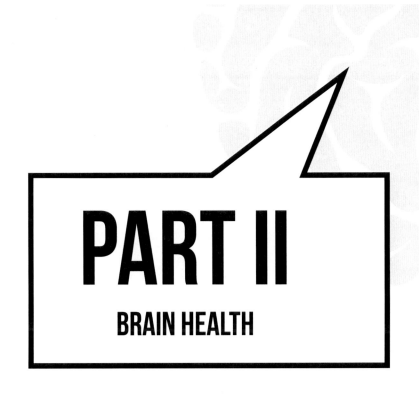

PART II

BRAIN HEALTH

If you don't take care of your body's physical needs, your brain will be in no condition to lead anyone, yourself included. As the saying goes, "Leadership is action, not position." (McGannon) And part of that action is taking care of yourself—and modeling self-care for those you lead.

The ability to successfully incorporate any of the lessons in this book into your personal or professional life will depend largely on your capacity to get enough sleep, activity and nutrition. That's what the first three lessons in this section of the book are all about. They are keystone habits that enable you to show up prepared to lead. These lessons are likely not anything you don't already know. However, it is very likely you may have forgotten them or have tricked yourself into believing that they somehow don't apply to you.

They do.

The following three lessons, in fact, are the most important of this entire book and some of the most important things that your mother ever taught you.

1

GO TO
BED

Like many people with a strong work ethic, I've been asked, "When do you sleep?" more often than I care to admit.

I can remember being asked that question as early as high school, when I was balancing two jobs (one was at a gas station that was open until midnight and the other—as a lifeguard—often involved the 6 a.m. "early bird" shift at the pool), playing sports, being social and maintaining good grades.

Fast-forward 25 years, and not much has changed. I still have a lot of balls in the air including my executive role, a family, continued studies, building and launching the eLeadership Academy, speaking nationally and internationally, and writing a book. I've worked many a late night to make it all happen while everyone else I knew was sleeping, and not a month goes by without hearing that question again from friends, colleagues or family. I've often told them that I've been blessed or cursed as someone with initiative and ideas.

There's no doubt that my strong work ethic has allowed me to achieve more than I envisioned for myself growing up, but it has often come at the cost of sleep. I used to joke that I was "cheating time" by doing much of my work while others were sleeping. Little did I know that I was actually cheating my own health.

Now, with an understanding of the neuroscience of sleep, I can clearly see how my sleep loss created situations in which I was not in the best mood, was not fully attentive, was prone to making mistakes, caught colds more readily, was sometimes forgetful, and, on occasion, developed a dreaded eye twitch—a tell-tale sign that I needed sleep. There were even a few situations when I had to roll down the car window, crank the music or simply pull over to the side of the road while driving because my need to sleep had overpowered my desire to stay awake. Sigh. There you have it … confessions of a sleep-deprived overachiever.

Sleep Deprivation and Performance

A National Sleep Foundation poll revealed that nearly two-thirds of Americans (63%) say their sleep needs are not being met during the week. The study also revealed that 60% of respondents experienced a sleep problem, such as waking during the night, waking too early or feeling un-refreshed when they get up in the morning, either every night or almost every night.[8] Based on these statistics, a larger percentage of people lacking quality sleep are coming to work than those who are consistently sleeping well. This is worrisome when you understand the impacts on performance and well-being.

Chances are, you already know that such widespread sleep deprivation cannot be without consequences. And you're right. A growing body of research shows just how important it is to keep our bodies and minds well rested. So why do so many of us continue to ignore our biology and burn the midnight oil?

Perhaps the biggest reason is that the consequences of sleep deprivation are, for the most part, invisible. While you can see a broken arm or a scraped knee, you can't see the devastating effects that sleep deprivation has on your brain. And believe me, they are devastating.

Sleep deprivation in the Western world is rampant—and has massive cognitive and overall health consequences. Sleep deprivation impedes judgment, lengthens reaction time and interferes with problem-solving.[9] When you lack sleep, you make more mistakes, you're more inclined to rely on your emotional brain rather than your thinking brain to respond to people and circumstances, and your ability to focus is severely impaired, which in turn impacts your memory retention.

As discussed, our biggest value proposition as leaders is our ability to think. And when we lack sleep, there are significant impacts on our ability to perform the task of thinking. Two of the most significant impacts are on learning and memory. We have difficulty digesting new information and consequently remembering what we've learned when tired.[10] When we sleep, our brain consolidates memories and learning in the mind.[11] When we cut ourselves short on sleep, therefore, how can we expect to remember anything? Think about when you're feeling on top of your game; you most likely remember names, tasks and other information more readily. When you feel tired, on the other hand, those otherwise simple tasks become much more difficult. Your brain feels sluggish.

All of this is extremely detrimental to our personal and organizational leadership impact.

Lack of sleep has played a role in some of the biggest disasters in our history, including the Exxon Valdez oil spill[12], the nuclear meltdown of Chernobyl[13] and the crash of American Airlines flight 1420.[14] Even more common, it plays a role in many smaller incidents in our day-to-day lives much more often than we may think.

Researchers from Uppsala University in Sweden have found that going without sleep for just one night causes changes in the brain similar to those that occur after receiving a blow to the head. In their study, otherwise healthy young men who skipped a night of sleep actually showed a spike in the chemicals NSE and S-100B, which are biomarkers for brain damage.[15]

How much sleep do you need? There are many opinions and recommendations on this topic, averaging around seven to eight hours per night. According to one report, "The best way to determine an individual's sleep needs is to go to bed when tired and sleepy, and to get up in the morning when feeling refreshed, without an alarm."[16] That sounds like something our mothers might say!

Sleep and Mood

If your mother was anything like mine, she likely told you at some point, "Go to bed or you'll be cranky in the morning!" We all know that sleep impacts our mood, yet we often forgo sleep to do something more "productive" while not planning for the negative impact on our mood the following day. We all have too much to do and too little time in which to do it. So, we stay up late to cram in a couple more hours of work or send a few emails from the comfort of a warm bed. Then we get up extra early to sneak in a workout before heading to the office to put the finishing touches on a report we need to present. We see these as victimless crimes. After all, what are we missing? It's only sleep, right?

Our mothers would disagree, and they have solid proof to back them up. Research has shown that sleep deprivation causes people to feel more stressed, angry, sad and mentally exhausted[17]. When we show up in the workplace like this we aren't doing anything good for ourselves, the customer, or the organization. When leaders show up cranky, this cascades to others (known as emotional contagion, which is discussed in Lesson 9) and a ripple of negativity ensues, leading to the epidemic of disengagement discussed in Part I of this book.

A Leader's Responsibility

Dr. Charles A. Czeisler, a professor of sleep medicine at Harvard Medical School, rather eloquently summed up the hypocrisy and irrationality of the Western world's glorification of sleep deprivation:

> Putting yourself or others at risk while driving or working at an impaired level is bad enough. Expecting your employees to do the same is just irresponsible. It amazes me that contemporary work and social culture glorifies sleeplessness in the way we once glorified people who could hold their liquor. It has been shown that 24 hours without sleep or a week of sleeping four or five hours a night prompts an impairment equal to a blood alcohol level of 0.1%. We would never say, 'This guy is drunk all the time, but he's a great worker!' yet we continue to acknowledge people who sacrifice sleep.18

Though most workplaces have strict rules against showing up at work drunk, our hectic workload and frantic pace of life encourage employees to show up every day in a similar state of inebriation.

As a leader, you need to recognize this and rise above it. Though it's hard to regulate the sleep habits of those you lead, you can at least ensure that you get adequate sleep every night and show up to work refreshed and ready to lead to your potential.

Doing this, of course, is more easily said than done. Most of the problem has to do with a lack of willpower. People forgo the long-term benefits of sleep for the short-term benefits of getting things done, socializing, or entertainment. My willpower is constantly tested with the temptation to do one more thing before I go to bed, or the urge to binge-watch the newest season of my favourite Netflix series.

The essence of emotional intelligence is being self-aware and taking personal responsibility for yourself and how you interact with others. Taking responsibility for getting enough sleep is part of good leadership. In other words, it's *your personal responsibility* to get enough sleep so that your mood doesn't negatively impact others.

Getting a good night's sleep makes a big difference in your personal well-being and cognitive performance. That's good news for you, those you lead, and your organization.

Melatonin and Screens

The chemical that your brain releases to make you feel relaxed, tired, and ultimately fall asleep is called melatonin. Melatonin is what controls your sleep/wake cycle, or circadian rhythm. It's important to realize that your body releases more melatonin in the evening, usually peaking around 2 a.m. Unfortunately, as we grow older, we produce and release less and less melatonin, making it increasingly challenging to get a good night's sleep.[19] Working with the natural melatonin rhythms of your body rather than against them will help you leverage the good work your brain is trying to do to help you get good rest. In other words, don't fight the urge to sleep and continue to stay up late. Go to bed, and your body—and brain—will thank you. Consider the onset of yawning a solid tell that it's time for bed. My mom always used to say, "Go to bed if you're tired."

Not only do we need to work with the natural rhythm of our bodies to produce and release melatonin, we also need to manage the forces working against it. Research has confirmed that the LED light—the bright glow rich in blue wavelengths from devices such as tablets, phones or computers, suppresses the release of melatonin.[20]

So, the next time you're lying in bed and you decide to check your email or scan your social feeds one more time, think about what your mom used to say about watching TV before bed—"It will keep you up." Are you sacrificing just a few minutes, or is it a few minutes plus the additional time it will take you to fall asleep thanks to the awakening glow of your device? Or is it all of that plus the negative consequences of sleep deprivation the next day?

Tips for Getting More Sleep:

A quick online search will yield thousands of results for how to get more sleep, but here are a few of my favourite quick tips that I've used to improve my own sleep and that will very likely work for you as well:

1. **Get comfortable** – A good bed, pillow and bedding can make a big difference.

2. **Darken the room** – When your body detects light, it naturally starts to wake. Having blackout curtains or blinds really helps keep the light out and can help you sleep. I discovered blackout curtains a few years ago, and using them has made a big difference in the quality of my sleep during the months when the sun rises earlier then I do.

3. **Limit screen time** – Minimize the use of electronic devices, including TV, near bedtime. Try reading on paper rather than on a screen.

4. **Have a routine** – Our minds love routines; they give us comfort. When you do the same things before bed each night, you signal your body that it's time to wind down.

5. **Watch what you eat and drink** – Eat just enough food to not be hungry while sleeping; too much food can make you have a restless sleep. Limit caffeine and alcohol, as they can cause difficulties sleeping. You'll also want to limit the amount of liquid you consume during the evening so you don't have to wake to go to the washroom.

6. **Don't nap after dinner** – You're better off keeping yourself awake after dinner and then going to bed a bit earlier. My mom always warned me in situations like this, "If you sleep now, you won't sleep later." This is something that I say to my husband at least once a week as his eyes close while he's lying on the couch after a hard day of work. Perhaps my next book will be called, "Your Wife was Right: 10 Lessons for a Successful Marriage." Insert smiley face here.

7. **Get exercise** – If you get exercise during the day (but not too close to bedtime), you'll burn energy and be more ready for bed.

8. **Deep breathing** – Spend a few minutes doing some deep-breathing exercises. The 4-7-8 relaxing breath exercise, described in detail in Lesson 12, is a great way to calm the mind and prepare yourself for a restful sleep.

The major takeaway is this: don't sacrifice long-term benefits of sleep for short-term gains. The impacts of sleep deprivation can span everything from moodiness to death, with some significant health impacts such as stroke, diabetes and heart disease in-between.[21] Even if your mother isn't there to tell you every night, it's still critically important that you go to bed.

2

GO
PLAY

My life choices have played havoc with my ingrained drive to be active. Growing up, I was always active. I was part of nearly every school sports team, I swam competitively, and I loved cross-country running. After post-secondary, I got married and started a family in my 20s. With most of my time dedicated to parenting and career, my activity level dropped substantially.

In my early 30s, I decided to accomplish some marathons and triathlons, so I made physical activity and training a priority—and I'd never felt better. On the flip side, in my 40s, I invested significant time in professional endeavours, such as furthering my education and career, building the online eLeadership Academy and, most recently, writing this book. Unfortunately, many of these things are done from a seated position. Although my hard work has enabled me to further my personal ambitions and impact, it has come at a cost.

During the periods of my life when I made physical activity a priority, I felt healthy, confident and capable. The reverse is also true; when I was not active, I felt less healthy, which led to less passion for and less confidence in all of my endeavours.

My life has been a constant trade-off between two ends of the spectrum. I have another young child now, and I often feel like I'm clinging to the swinging end of a pendulum or desperately trying to hold onto one end of a teeter-totter that's gone *awry! It's all so rewarding, yet exhausting, and it leaves little time for self-care. If you've experienced parenthood, I'm pretty confident you can relate.*

My studies have provided compelling evidence that lack of activity is bad for the brain— and remind me of the importance of prioritising an active lifestyle.

Strengthen Your Brain with Physical Activity

Does your day look anything like this? You sit working at a computer for eight hours a day, then go home and sit some more because you're exhausted from using your brain all day. Instead of getting active—which would do your body and your brain a whole lot of good—you turn on the TV, grab your laptop, phone or tablet or do some other sedentary activity that makes you feel comfortable and lets your brain relax after a mentally taxing day at the office. If this sounds like you, then you're like me and many other 21ˢᵗ-century workers. And this next bit is going to sound like a bit of tough love from our mothers: our sedentary lifestyle is killing us!

Sitting isn't good for our physical health, but it has particularly adverse effects on the brain. When we are sitting, our bodies do not require as much fuel, and the extra glucose in our system contributes to diabetes, obesity, heart disease and other problems.[22]

Have you seen Disney-Pixar movie *WALL-E*, which depicts future humans who are overweight and do not have the ability to think for themselves? If not, check it out. It's an endearing movie about friendship, the environment and the power of humanity, yet it runs unnervingly parallel to the current-day challenges of obesity and cognitive decline as a result of our sedentary lifestyles.

Here's the thing: your brain isn't best served by relaxing after sitting all day; it *needs* you to get active. Being active promotes a process known as neurogenesis, which is the brain's ability to grow new brain cells, regardless of age.[23] Since the human brain starts losing nerve tissue around age 30, this is particularly pertinent to many of us who are in leadership positions today. We need all the brain cells we can get!

Brain science, in fact, has been linking exercise to brain health for many years. The way exercise directly improves brain health is fascinating. When you start exercising, your brain interprets it as a threat to your well-being, so the oldest part of your brain that houses the amygdala kicks in with its fight-or-flight mechanism (more on this in Part III). This is because in our earliest years as a species, running was not exercise—it was a means to escape being eaten for lunch by some kind of animal. As your heart rate goes up, your brain thinks you are either fighting or fleeing from an enemy. To protect you and your brain, your brain releases a protein known as BDNF (Brain-Derived Neurotrophic Factor), which both guards and repairs your brain while also acting as a sort of "reset switch." The more intense the exercise, the more BDNF is released.[24] More BDNF for me, please!

Research has proven that an active lifestyle over the course of a lifetime can lead to improved cognitive performance when compared to a sedentary lifestyle. Tests have shown that exercisers outperform couch potatoes in memory, attention, reasoning and problem solving.[25]

In addition to the cognitive benefits of exercise, leading an active lifestyle can actually improve the brain's ability to maintain itself physiologically. For example, research shows that people who exercise regularly have larger volumes of grey matter in the hippocampus, a region of the brain that's important for memory.[26]

Learning why activity is so important for brain health and cognition has been a source of motivation for me to make activity a priority in my life.

Exercise and Your Mood

The benefits of exercise don't end with physiology and cognitive function; exercise is also crucial to your mental health. This is something that's becoming more and more of an issue in our desk-bound, information-based and increasingly sedentary society. Unfortunately, it's expected that mental health issues like depression and anxiety will surpass heart disease in North America as the number one health challenge by the year 2030.[27] Yikes! You don't need to be a neuroscientist to see the correlation between the sedentary lifestyles we live because of work and technology, the exponential rise in mental health related diseases, the rise in disengagement, and the associated personal and organizational costs.

An Australian study published in the *American Journal of Preventative Medicine* studied the habits of 9,000 women between the ages of 50 and 55. The goal was to determine the effects of prolonged sitting and lack of exercise on depression. Researchers found that women who sat for more than seven hours a day had a 47% greater risk of depression than those who sat for less than four hours a day. Those who didn't participate in *any* activity had a 99% higher risk of developing depression than women who exercised.[28] That is plausible evidence to get us off our butts!

Lack of activity can kick off a vicious downward spiral that's hard to break. I can attest to this. You don't make time to be active because of all of the other priorities in your life; you don't feel like getting out and being active, so you don't. And then things start to snowball. You start tumbling down the rabbit hole of believing you should forgo being active in an effort to accomplish the work at hand, only to find out that the work never really gets done. In the end you just feel worse. The pattern of non-activity becomes more and more difficult to break because you feel less and less motivated.

Understanding what's going on in the brain can help you break this self-defeating pattern. We know that exercise stimulates the release of "feel good" chemicals and neurotransmitters like oxytocin, serotonin, dopamine and endorphins, which make you feel happy.[29] Exercise has been said to be a key weapon against depression. Some studies have even found it to be an alternative to antidepressant drugs for improving mood and well-being.[30]

It's great to know that by simply putting one foot in front of the other, our body releases chemicals in our brains to make us feel better.

Activity = Insight

Have you ever had the experience that your best ideas come when you're being active? It's not uncommon for runners—myself included—to say they do their best thinking, and come up with their best ideas, while out on the trails or pounding the pavement! Neuroscientists have confirmed this, citing that creativity increases by 60% when we're active.[31] The same study found that "walking opens up the free flow of ideas, and it is a simple and robust solution to the goals of increasing creativity and increasing physical activity."

Not only does activity lead to better ideas, it actually improves learning and memory. Studies have shown that the prefrontal cortex (PFC), the thinking part of the brain, has greater volume in people who are regularly active compared to those who are not.[32] Another study done by researchers at the University of British Columbia found that sweat gland activity increases the size of the hippocampus, the part of the brain responsible for memory and learning.[33] Research by Dr. Kirk Erickson of the University of Pittsburgh found that seniors between the ages of 60 and 80 who walked for 30 to 45 minutes three days a week for one year saw hippocampus growth of up to 2%.[34] That's not too bad considering we're looking at an aging population more accustomed to experiencing brain shrinkage than brain growth.

Cognitive Disease

The most compelling evidence for me to put exercise on my priority list came when I learned about the rapid increase in dementia worldwide. Dementia is the term used to describe a range of symptoms associated with cognitive decline in memory or other thinking skills that impact a person's ability to do everyday tasks. Alzheimer's disease is the most widely known form of dementia, accounting for 60-80% of all cases.[35]

Devastatingly, a new case of dementia is diagnosed every few seconds around the world. In 2015, it was estimated that over 46 million people were living with dementia worldwide, and that this number is estimated to increase to 131.5 million by 2050.[36] The economic and social impact of dementia is already significant, but there are signs that we can positively influence this worrisome trend.

Evidence suggests that physical activity may reduce the impacts of cognitive function loss associated with Alzheimer's[37], and reduce age-related cognitive decline.[38]

Personally, I've seen how dementia steals a person's life. It's a tragedy for the person experiencing it and for those who love them. It breaks my heart to see a person with dementia become a shell of their former self, unable to connect with the people around them, and to see the impact on the families who love them. I'm willing to do just about anything I can to avoid putting my own loved ones through this, and that includes scheduling a few hours of exercise each week.

There is so much more research to be done to uncover how we can fight back and stop the staggering increase of dementia cases worldwide. In the meantime, the research I've outlined regarding the importance of being active to increase cognitive performance, improve overall health, and ward off age-related brain disease is encouraging. I strongly believe that this is one of the most important takeaways I can leave you with: *you can improve your cognitive performance and lessen your likelihood of age-related cognitive decline just by being active.* From a personal and organizational leadership perspective, what could be more important?

Just Do It

I know; there are so many things you need to do, and so many demands for your time and attention, that it's hard to find the time and energy to exercise. I get it—I just don't accept it as an excuse. We are all busy, but as our mothers said, "Where there is a will, there is a way." We all have time that can be carved out of our daily routines for exercise, but we have to choose to allocate that time to activity that matters. Do you "unwind" in front of the TV after a day of work, or do you recharge your batteries with a revitalizing half-hour walk or run? Do you drive to and from work each day, or do you walk or bike to work and arrive mentally invigorated and ready to face the day? We all choose to be, or not to be, active. Even giving up 15 minutes of TV or Internet browsing a day could make a big impact.

Maybe your job requires you to sit for most of the day. While you may not be able to slip away from the office at lunch and go for a run, there are still things you can do at work to minimize the adverse effects of sitting. Here are some ideas:

1. Use your coffee or lunch breaks to go for a walk.

2. Get up from your desk and walk around the office once every hour.

3. Go talk to people rather than phoning, emailing or texting them.

4. Send files to a printer that's on the other side of the office so you have to walk to get your documents, and try standing up while talking on the phone.

5. Use a pair of work pants as your barometer. I have one pair of dress pants that I've kept for over a decade. Every few months I wear them to determine how I'm doing. If they are a little tight, I know that pendulum has swung too far in the direction of unhealthy. When they feel comfortable again, I know that things are back on track.

There are great phone apps and wearable devices that can remind you to get active, as well as several new innovations to help you avoid the dreaded effects of sitting. A few years ago, I purchased a device that allows me to convert my workspace into a stand-up desk and alternate between sitting and standing as often as I like. It cost a few hundred dollars but was worth every penny. Recently, I have seen some other great solutions for this kind of functionality. Google "cardboard box standing desk" for ideas that require little or no investment.

If you are looking for a good workplace program to get you and your team moving, check out the Virgin Pulse Global Challenge. It's a worldwide online program that has had over 2 million participants, and it's a great solution to get a baseline of your team's well-being. The cornerstone of the challenge is a 100-day journey in teams of seven with a focus on improving activity, sleep, nutrition and more. Being responsible for human resources for an organization, and having participated a few times myself, I can tell you that it's a cost-effective solution for improving knowledge of these important areas that our mothers warned us about. The team aspect of the challenge keeps participants accountable for their steps. My team won the last challenge, and I'm just about to embark with six other colleagues on the next 100-day journey!

Everyone's situation is different, but I know there are little things you can do that will get you up and moving during and after work hours. It's really up to you to take action. As mentioned in the onset of this section, leadership is action, not position.

Where to Play

If your mom is like mine, she often didn't stop at "Go play!" She'd send you all the way out the front door to play *outside*, and once again, she has science to back her up. There's a plurality of evidence showing that, if you have the choice, being active outdoors is better for you than being active indoors. Outdoor activity has been proven to help clear your mind, improve your mood, spur creativity and problem-solving, lower stress and blood pressure, and even improve immunity.[39] Interestingly, the first five minutes of being active outside has the biggest impact, which gives more credence to the notion of "something is better than nothing."[40]

Our mothers warned us that sitting around isn't good for us, so, "Go play!"

3

YOU ARE WHAT
YOU EAT

A few years ago, I watched some documentaries about the quality of the food that we eat and its impact on our health. One of them outlined what really goes on inside industrial-scale feedlots and showed how most meat is processed. Yuck. I was appalled by the condition of the animals and concerned about the health implications that were being reported about meat and dairy within a human diet. I was confused and concerned, so I decided to cut out meat altogether.

I'd never been a big foodie anyway, so I wouldn't really miss it, right? What's the worst that could happen? I cut out meat without giving it much thought. It wasn't until about a year later that I started to notice symptoms I couldn't explain.

At first, it was hard to focus in meetings. Sometimes I was seeing double. I noticed that I wasn't able to concentrate, and I was having difficulty remembering names. One day while doing a training session for a small group of people, I felt like the room was spinning and I needed to sit down. I was really perplexed by what was happening to me.

When I noticed that my heart was racing on a daily basis, I began to worry. At one point my heart was beating so fast that I went to see a doctor because I thought I was having heart issues. To my surprise, I learned I was very deficient in iron, and the perplexing symptoms were largely a result of my decision to eliminate meat *from my diet without including iron-rich foods in other ways. I affectionately refer to this time in my life as when I was a junk-food vegetarian.*

Through iron-rich foods, some supplements, and small solutions—such as using a cast iron frying pan for cooking—it has taken a few years to get my iron levels up to a level that is considered normal. The worrisome symptoms have disappeared, but if I don't pay attention to nutrition, my iron drops and the symptoms begin to percolate again. I hadn't known that making one decision based on my beliefs and values—not wanting to support factory farming—could so significantly impact my cognitive performance and overall health and well-being.

Fueling Our Brains

You already know that the human body needs food to fuel itself. What you might not realize is just how great an effect your nutritional choices can have on your *brain*. The food you eat is directly related to your ability to focus and be productive. Or maybe you know that, but you're so caught up in your busy schedule day-in-and-day-out that you don't have time to think about proper nutrition. You grab a bagel at the drive-thru on the way to work. You use coffee for a quick pick-me-up, or you grab some chocolate in the afternoon for a sugar fix. You'll eat better when you're less busy, you tell yourself. But then you never get less busy. I admit, there have been times when this has been me.

A study done by the International Labour Office concluded that 46% of all disease and 60% of all deaths were attributable to diet-related causes. Yikes! The global burden of diet-related diseases is expected to climb to 57% by 2020.[41] And if that doesn't motivate you to put down the bag of potato chips and pick up a banana, here's one more: you're 66% more likely to be less productive than someone who opts for a banana.[42]

If you've ever felt tired or sluggish after eating a big lunch, then you already know your food choices can do more than just make you feel full—they can affect your performance. The lack of certain nutrients is even thought to be toxic to the brain—especially in the elderly—and under-nutrition has been linked to processes that predispose the brain to shrinkage.[43]

As discussed, the brain generally shrinks with age unless we are proactive with things like sleep and exercise. Nutrition is another ally against age-related brain shrinkage. A lack of certain nutrients in an aging brain can lead to accelerated shrinkage and even death of brain cells. Scary stuff. The good news is that healthy habits such as physical activity and calorie restriction have been associated with neurogenesis (brain growth) and a larger hippocampus.[44]

Is that second bowl of ice cream really worth it?

The Cost of Poor Eating Habits

According to the World Health Organization (WHO), an estimated 30% of the world's population is iron-deficient, which can reduce performance and physical work capacity—and suggests that adequate nutrition could boost national productivity by 20%.[45] Given my own experience with iron deficiency and the effect it had on my ability to think, I can certainly attest to the cost of poor eating habits.

But, it sometimes seems like the deck is stacked against us. Our culture encourages us to work harder and longer, which has been chewing away not only at our sleep and physical activity but also at our nutrition. Instead of cooking healthily and eating slowly, we eat on the run, grabbing pre-packaged servings of food-like substances that are genetically and chemically engineered to be irresistible—often through the addition of unhealthy amounts of salt and sugar.

When you combine being inactive with poor food choices, it's no wonder that obesity is escalating. In the United States alone, more than two-thirds of the population is overweight or obese.[46] Canada is similar with a study indicating that 62% of men and 46% of women are either overweight or obese.[47]

Food and Your Mood

There is considerable research linking a poor diet to a range of health issues such as diabetes, obesity, heart disease and cancer. There is no doubt that a poor diet has a harmful long-term effect on our overall well-being. But what about the short-term effects? Does our diet impact our mood and the way we show up personally and professionally? Although there is less scientific evidence to cite on this topic, most of us intuitively know it to be true. Most of us understand, for example, what it means to be "h-angry." Meaning, when we are hungry, we get grumpy, or angry. You think it would be common sense to eat when you are hungry, but unfortunately many of us fall victim to that one-more-thing-to-do trap before we eat. This doesn't bode well for those we lead.

There is some research that shows that a poor diet can make us feel worse, and even heighten symptoms of depression. A study reported in the British Journal of Psychiatry, for example, found that a diet of processed foods can increase the likelihood of depression within five years, while a diet based on whole foods can help ward off depression.[48]

Unfortunately, like sleep deprivation and lack of activity, food and mood can often become entangled in a sort of vicious downward spiral, particularly when we mix in stress or anxiety. Research has shown that when we are stressed, we eat more food, and we choose foods higher in calories.[49] This is because persistent stress increases the level of cortisol in our bloodstream, which increases appetite and motivation to eat. The high-fat, high-sugar "comfort foods" we reach for when stressed may comfort us in the short term, but they do little for our overall ability to think and well-being in the long run. (Unfortunately for women, research suggests that women are more inclined than men to make poor food choices and suffer the corresponding weight gain.[50])

So, which foods should we be choosing?

When it comes to nutrition, there is so much information on diet that it's overwhelming. I recommend you talk with a professional such as your doctor or a nutritionist about what's best for you. I can share that, when it comes to the brain, recent research has found that diets high in vegetables, fruits, unprocessed grains, omega-3 fatty acids (found in foods like fish, walnuts and kiwis), and that contain only modest amounts of lean meats and dairy, are good for the brain.[51] Deficiencies in omega-3 fatty acids have been linked to numerous cognitive disorders, including dementia, depression, attention-deficit disorder, dyslexia, bipolarism and schizophrenia.[52] Keep an eye out for new research in this area as it seems that neuroscientists are routinely discovering new truths and debunking old ones.

Another way your diet can influence your mood is through serotonin. About 95% of your serotonin—a neurotransmitter that, among other functions, helps mediate moods—is produced in your gut and is influenced by the amount of good bacteria in your gut.[53] Fortunately, the foods you eat can help cultivate a new microbiota (the good bacteria). Some good gut-bacteria foods include bananas, blueberries, broccoli, kale and beans.

Poor nutrition inevitably leads to suboptimal performance, which then impacts other aspects of our well-being, including sleep, stress and activity. Self-esteem also makes a difference in how we show up in terms of our personal and organizational leadership. To be completely frank, when we eat poor quality food, we feel terrible. When we don't feel good about ourselves, we feel less confident, and our ability to effectively lead ourselves and others declines.

Healthier Eating at Work

The evidence couldn't be any clearer. You, your employees, and your colleagues are not only susceptible to poor performance due to inadequate nutrition; you're also at risk of weight gain and a host of related health problems and expenses. Because so many of us spend a large chunk of our lives at work, the office is a good place to start when it comes to making smarter nutritional choices.

Here are some thoughts on how to eat right at work:

1. **Plan your meals and snacks** – Take time the night before or in the morning to plan your lunch and snacks. Being prepared will save you the temptation of making poor choices when feeling stressed and hungry.

2. **Keep coffee to a minimum** – Many workplaces offer endless amounts of coffee, and the temptation can be strong, especially when you feel sluggish or stressed. Drinking coffee all day can leave you jittery and dehydrated, and if you're adding cream and sugar each time, you're also adding a whole lot of empty calories.

3. **Stay hydrated** – Most adults are dehydrated to some degree. Even mild dehydration makes it difficult to think. Keep a bottle of water at your desk and try

adding some fresh fruit to make it more interesting!

4. **Be mindful of how much you eat** – Aim for balance and moderation. We live in a super-sized society, in which most restaurants serve meals way larger than we need. A lighter lunch will help prevent a blood-sugar drop in the afternoon and help you maintain your focus.

5. **Take a break to eat** – As a final note, step away from your desk and allow yourself time to eat without working. Trying to multitask will only lead to poorer food choices and overeating.

If you want your brain to function at its best, you need to give some thought to what you are feeding it. Eating right affects your ability to sleep well, focus, maintain a good mood, think clearly and generally feel great.

Remember what your mother said: "You are what you eat."

NOTES FOR PART II

I want to remember:

_____

I want to stop:

_____

I want to start:

_____

The biggest thing preventing me from taking action is:

_____

I plan to overcome this by:

_____

Two things I will do are:

1. _____

2. _____

The day I will start is:

_____

PART III

RESPONDING TO THREAT

The human brain is hardwired to anticipate danger and react quickly to threats whether real or perceived. When early humans were hunting and scavenging, they had to be constantly aware of their surroundings; although they wanted to catch something big and tasty for dinner, they could just as easily have ended up as someone or something else's dinner.

That's why we've evolved to recognize things that break an expected pattern, seem out of place, or otherwise just don't seem quite right. Some things simply feel "creepy." We've all heard that clichéd expression, "It's quiet—too quiet." When our early ancestors stepped out onto the plains to hunt and realized the usual chirping and calling of birds overhead was absent, they knew that a predator hidden in the tall grass may very well be the reason for the silence.

Our instincts evolved for a reason—to keep us alive. The problem is that many of the threats that necessitated such evolutionary adaptation simply don't exist anymore in the modern world, or at least not nearly to the extent they did long ago. The famous "fight-or-flight response" is a vital instinct that can keep us alive in a pinch. But in today's world, it's much more often an inappropriate overreaction to something that's probably not nearly as threatening as our primitive brain thinks it is.

Whether the fight-or-flight response is triggered by a bear in the woods or an overbearing boss, the physiological response is the same. The activity of the hypothalamus—the pearl-sized part of the brain that's responsible for initiating a sequence of chemical releases and nerve cell firings that prepares us for running or fighting—is summed up quite succinctly by Dr. Neil Neimark:

> When our fight or flight response is activated, sequences of nerve cell firing occur and chemicals like adrenaline, noradrenaline and cortisol are released into our bloodstream. These patterns of nerve cell firing and chemical release cause our body to undergo a series of very dramatic changes. Our respiratory rate increases. Blood is shunted away from our digestive tract and directed into our muscles and limbs, which require extra energy and fuel for running and fighting. Our pupils dilate. Our awareness intensifies. Our sight sharpens. Our impulses quicken. Our perception of pain diminishes. Our immune system mobilizes with increased activation. We become prepared—physically and psychologically—for fight or flight. We scan and search our environment, "looking for the enemy."[54]

That constant scanning of our environment for "the enemy" can cause very real problems in a world where actual enemies are few and far between. This unceasing vigilance, in fact, leads to a "negativity bias," the psychological phenomenon by which humans pay more attention to and give more weight to negative rather than positive experiences or other kinds of information.
From a survival perspective, it makes sense that we would be more tuned in to things that could hurt us. But, negativity bias can have an insidious effect on leadership when we overreact to threats (perceived or real) as a result of our fight-or-flight response.[55]

4

IT'S NOT THE END
OF THE WORLD

The end-is-near feeling has been in the air more often than I would like to re-member in my twenty-year career in the financial services industry. Changing regulations, declining profits, disruptive employees, or customers threatening legal action have evoked worst-case scenario thinking and unnecessary stress for myself and others. Looking back, I can see how I underestimated the resilience of people to get through any situation and could have saved myself and others a lot of grief had I focused more on what was probable and possible.

Unfortunately, as a bit of a worrier, I anticipate dangers way more often than they actually happen—at a ratio that I'd not care to admit. With a better understanding of the brain, I've learned why I've been anticipating the pitfalls of everything that could possibly go wrong, how it's not serving me, and strategies to focus less on the possible negative outcomes and more on the desired positive outcomes.

In response to my worry when I was growing up, my mother often said to me, "It's not the end of the world." She meant that whatever happened, or whatever I was anticipating happening, wasn't really as bad as I thought it was. As usual, she was right.

Negativity Bias

While perceiving danger around every corner may have kept our primitive ancestors alive, it's more likely these days to get in the way of our ability to trust, stay positive, and move forward. *The technical term for our inclination to anticipate the worst is called "negativity bias."* From a leadership perspective, anticipating threats is important, but if it becomes more of the focus than fostering hope, relationships, and traction to achieve goals, then a team or workplace becomes a very depressing place full of fear and pessimism.

Unfortunately, there are people who lead by fear and take every opportunity to point out the worst-case scenario to others. This type of leadership evokes a threat response in those they lead, which releases the stress hormones of cortisol and adrenaline, which narrows the ability to think and be positive. The result is a downward spiral of engagement, trust, teamwork, and buy-in. When we are operating in a situation of perceived threat, our brain functions very differently than when we feel security, trust and hope. This is the difference between fear-based leadership and hope-based leadership. When seeking engagement for ourselves and those we lead, hope-based leadership is the best option.

The primary function of our brain is to avoid danger and seek reward—in that order. We're drawn to bad news like a moth to a flame because the most primitive part of our brain is clamouring for attention, screaming, "Look at that! What is it? Is it dangerous?!"

News publishers eager to sell more copies or entice more views of their stories recognized the powerful effects of negativity bias long ago, which is why journalists are intimately familiar with the old adage, "If it bleeds, it leads."

The power of negative events or experiences goes much deeper than newspaper headlines. A paper published in the Review of General Psychology described how "bad emotions, bad parents, and bad feedback have more impact than good ones, and bad information is processed more thoroughly than good."[56] Bad impressions and stereotypes form more quickly than good ones and are harder to change.

In fact, the paper's authors found "hardly any exceptions" to the phenomenon of "bad" being more powerful than "good," remarking that, "Taken together, these findings suggest that bad is stronger than good, as a general principle across a broad range of psychological phenomena."[57]

We really don't need research to confirm this. We know this. Unfortunately, many of the bad experiences I've had as a leader have etched their way into my memory much more deeply than the good ones. Those I work with have often heard me refer to these bad-experience memories as my battle scars. My battle scars are many and well-earned, and they serve as caution flags when I find myself in a similar situation that isn't going as well as I'd previously hoped or expected. They remind me of what not to do so that I don't fall into the same pitfall that I did the previous time. My battle scars include everything from comments that were well intended but taken the wrong way, change that was put forward without understanding the full impact, or losing my cool when challenged by those who seemed ungrateful or indifferent to the effort I felt that I had exerted on their behalf.

Although I may not remember each of the negative moments in detail, flags go up in my mind when I recognize a situation is similar to a past situation where things went sideways. Past experience shapes our perspective and our reactions. But, while warning flags serve us in terms of not making the same mistake twice, they also limit our willingness to try something new and trust that things could be different this time. Effective leaders understand that just because it didn't go as planned the last time, doesn't mean that it won't go differently this time. They use their experience as a basis to navigate a new way forward.

Catastrophizing and Rumination

If you still find yourself wondering what's so bad about being drawn to negative information, you should be warned that negativity bias will commonly lead you into a couple of emotional and leadership traps.

The first is known as *catastrophizing*—where you expect the worst and spend your time focusing on worst-case scenarios. While it's important to be prepared for any possible situation, dwelling on these catastrophic outcomes until they seem almost inevitable is not an emotionally healthy way to go through life. Catastrophizing can also manifest itself in the way you respond to events that have already occurred. "Why does this always happen to me?" "This is the worst day ever!" "Things will never be ok again." These are all examples of catastrophizing.

The second trap is *rumination*, which is the compulsion to focus on the negative or threatening aspects of a situation that has already occurred, rather than letting go, moving on or seeking solutions. It means dwelling on what you could have or should have said or done even though you have no way of changing the past. Rumination is similar to worry, except that rumination is dwelling on the past, whereas worry is being concerned about things that could happen in the future. Both can be attributed to our propensity to expect the worst, which unfortunately often leads to anxiety, stress, and decreased emotional well-being.

Once you understand the concept of negativity bias and the fact that you or those you lead might be inclined to catastrophize or ruminate to anticipate and mitigate potential threats, you can work to minimize these time-sucking and stressful habits. When I catch myself fearing the worst (catastrophizing), or playing a scenario over and over in my head about what I could have done or should have said (ruminating), I recognize what is happening and logically know it's my negativity bias. I also know that this type of thinking is not serving me, so I work on changing my focus by redirecting my attention to something else, or asking myself questions like, "What's the opportunity here?" "How can I think differently about this?" or "How likely is the worst-case scenario to happen?"

I've also found that getting some sleep helps. I can be worked up about something, and after a night's sleep, or even a quick nap, it's usually not that important or worrisome anymore. Returning to the basics of Part II is often the best path forward—get some sleep, go for a run, or feed your brain something nutritious. Doing nothing to change focus, and continuing to catastrophize or ruminate in these kinds of situations, isn't effective. Each person's technique to change their focus in these situations might be different. The important part is to catch yourself in these patterns and find what works best for you to redirect your attention. As our mothers advised, "Get over it," or "Move on."

Negativity bias and fear-of-the-worst is most prominent for me when there is seemingly something to worry about for my own personal health or the health of someone I love. Just recognizing this about myself has been a powerful lever for change in these situations. In Mom's next lesson—"Use your words!"—you'll learn a strategy to calm the threat response in situations such as this when negativity bias is strong.

The good news is that, with practise, it gets easier to stop these unproductive and stress-inducing patterns. When we understand why we do something, we are more equipped to make the needed changes. I've also found that by introducing the concepts to those you lead and work with, it will serve to help the group have a common language to support each other to move on and not focus on the negative.

Robert Hargrove, author of one of my favourite leadership books, *Masterful Coaching*, offers a powerful metaphor to depict the kinds of stories we tell ourselves.[58] It has stuck with me, so I'll pass it along here in hope that it has the same impact on you. Hargrove says that we tell ourselves stories based on our interpretation of what happened, and if we let our negativity bias taint our view, the stories are most often "rut" stories, where we feel stuck and like a victim of the circumstance. On the other hand, when we can see past the danger or threat of what's wrong or what could go wrong, we tell ourselves "river" stories—where optimism, hope and solutions flow. What kind of stories do you tell yourself most often, "river" stories or "rut" stories? We'll talk more about mindset in Lesson #13 when we take an in-depth look at Mom's advice to "Change your attitude!"

The Bright Side of Negativity Bias

To be clear, negativity bias—or expecting the worst—isn't always a bad thing. Take, for instance, what happened to a colleague of mine. While sitting at his desk, he suddenly heard the screeching of tires coming from the direction of the normally quiet street beyond his office window. Rather than ignore the sound, a quick look confirmed that a truck was out of control, and he instinctively moved himself to the back wall of his office—the wall furthest away from the street. A few seconds later, the truck smashed through his window and ended up nearly on top of his desk, right where he'd been sitting not a moment earlier. Had his amygdala, with its bias for negativity, not been scanning for danger and ensuring that his instinctive reaction was the safest one, he might not be here today. Instead, he walked away from the harrowing experience without a physical scratch.

Expecting things that could go wrong has served me well in terms of being prepared, especially when it comes to speaking engagements. Every time I prepare for a speaking engagement I go through a mental list of all the things that could go wrong, such as presentation files not working, technology not working, poor audio, going over time, or possible wardrobe malfunctions. In reality, I've had all of those things happen at one time or another, but, by anticipating what could go wrong, I've been able to plan well to mitigate challenges and deliver most presentations without incident. If managed correctly, your negativity bias can help you prepare for challenges and pitfalls, be adaptable, and keep yourself free of physical harm when need be.

Drivers of Threat Responses

The challenge of living with negativity bias at work is that we often feel under "threat" because of the stress that is prevalent in our workplace. Our brains are "dialed in" to the action and behaviour of those around us, who all too often trip our hair-trigger threat response system.

"Dr. David Rock coined the term 'Neuroleadership' and is the Director of the NeuroLeadership Institute, a global initiative bringing neuroscientists and leadership experts together to build a new science for leadership development."[59] If you find the connection between the brain and leadership of interest, I encourage you to check out more of David Rock's work—he is a pioneer and thought leader in the area of Neuroleadership.

Rock identifies five drivers of our threat-reward response, which he refers to with the acronym SCARF: status, certainty, autonomy, relatedness and fairness.[60] How a situation impacts these drivers dictates whether the brain perceives the situation as a threat or a potential reward.

Negativity bias often leads to the perception that social slights are everywhere. That's why when a coworker passes you in the hall and casually says, "Nice shirt," it's very hard to simply accept the compliment without first agonizing over whether it was sincere or sarcastic. By default, your brain interprets the remark as a potential shot at your status and your threat response kicks in. Perhaps you become consciously aware of every glance cast your way for the rest of day, which greatly limits your ability to focus on producing quality work.

This is further amplified if you've had a negative interaction with this person in the past that has triggered a threat response. A simple example, but you can imagine the impact on engagement and well-being if this perception of threat happens frequently. As Mom suggested, "Don't get your back up." Instead, try to "Get that chip off your shoulder."

Seeing the Glass as Half Full

In his book, *The Happiness Advantage*, Shawn Achor coins the term "The Positive Tetris Effect" to describe a process of training your brain to see the positive in situations.[61] The term comes from research done on people who played the Tetris game so much that they began to see Tetris shapes wherever they looked. Our brain is always looking for efficiency to conserve energy, which is why it looks for patterns. Like those who see Tetris shapes in the world as a result of frequently playing the game, it's possible to train the brain to see the good in situations rather than the bad. Here's an easy way to test that theory. Look around you and notice everything that is black. Now close your eyes. Can you remember the things that are green in the area you looked? Likely not, because your brain filtered out all of the other colours based on your intent to only see black. Once you know this, you can train your brain to filter out the negative, and see the positive.

When faced with something that has you fearing the worst, ask yourself, "What's the silver lining in this situation? What's the opportunity? How can I think differently about this?" There are always valuable lessons with every change, problem or difficulty. It often takes effort to identify them, but it gets easier with practise. By seeing the glass as half full, you can calm the instinctive fight-or-flight response. Try it! It's a powerful way to keep your negativity bias in check. Here are some other ideas to help manage emotions:

1. **Build trusting relationships with colleagues and friends.** In a busy world, full of technology that gets in the way of face-to-face relationships, this takes some effort. It's worth the effort. When we feel trust, we are less likely to feel threatened and expect the worst.

2. **Manage your expectations.** Recognize how often you are disappointed in the actions of others and recognize that you can't control others; you

can only control yourself. If your expectations are constantly not being met, you are destined to only see what's not working. Focus on what you can do in the situation and how you want to show up rather than focusing on the actions or inactions of others.

3. **Focus on what you are grateful for.** Sometimes things do not go our way, but in every case, we can at least be grateful that we are alive—and there is opportunity to be grateful for so much more. Practise gratitude by identifying three things you are grateful for each day, and either write them down or share them with someone. There is a lot of research on the cognitive benefits of practising gratitude, and simple strategies exist for you and your team. Google has lots of information on the topic if you would like to explore further.

Bottom line: accept that you are hardwired to expect the worst. This instinct is essential for your survival, but in your leadership role, use the strategies above to focus on what's right or what's possible.

It's easy to get caught up in a negative mindset; indeed, your brain evolved to do just that. It's important to remember what Mom said: "It's not the end of the world."

Because she was right.

5

USE YOUR
WORDS

Throughout my career there have been many times when I've felt frustrated. Truth be told, nothing gets my back up more at work than negative or ungrateful co-workers and the prevalence of entitlement that many people have in the work-place. Even before studying neuroscience, I had intuitively learned that talking about my feelings when frustrated, angry, or hurt helps me feel calmer, more understanding, and more capable of moving forward. I've learned that there is always another perspective to consider and not everyone values the same things. Talking about what I'm feeling helps me. When I have felt challenged by ungrate-fulness or entitlement, I have learned to talk about it with trusted confidants, which lessens my emotional response and leads to better thinking about the prob-lem or opportunity at hand.

From a leadership perspective, I've also learned that getting others to talk about what they are feeling is good for their well-being and performance. For the last decade, I have worked to build coaching capabilities in myself and others. This included being certified as an executive coach, building a coaching culture at work, and building coaching into the eLeadership Academy. A threat response of some sort is usually the catalyst for a coaching conversation for me as a coachee or for those I coach.

I've learned that the coach approach—the practice of asking others what they think, rather than telling them what you think they should do—gives them an

opportunity to talk about what they are thinking. I've also found that most peo-
ple, including myself, speak-to-think (rather than think-to-speak), and that our
feelings become clearer when we talk about them. Giving people a chance to talk
about what they are feeling—followed by a plan that they devise for how to move
forward—is an effective leadership strategy.

Labeling Emotions

Labeling our emotions is known by psychologists as "affect labeling," and it is a good strategy for calming an emotional brain that is running amuck. Daniel Siegel, a professor of clinical psychology at UCLA and director of the Mindsight Institute, has created a clever and simple way of reminding us how right our mothers were about using our words. He calls it "name it to tame it." Research has shown that when we use our words to identify how we are feeling—either spoken internally to ourselves or out loud—we engage our thinking brain to label the emotion. The action of engaging the thinking brain helps calm the emotional brain, which helps regulate our emotional reaction and allows space for clearer thinking to prevail.

Renowned psychologist and neuroscientist, Dr. Matthew Lieberman, explored the effect of verbalizing emotions as a means to regulate behaviour in a fascinating article titled, *The Brain's Braking System (and how to 'use your words' to tap into it).*[62] In the article, Lieberman writes:

> As students improve in their ability and tendency to use emotional words to describe their feelings, they evidence fewer emotional outbursts and gain a range of benefits from classroom popularity to better academic performance.

Lieberman's article starts with an exploration of studies of various forms of self-control, including cognitive, emotional, financial, perspective-taking and motor. By studying the brain activity of participants hooked up to functional magnetic resonance imaging (fMRI), researchers have isolated the part of the PFC that's responsible for self-control—namely the *right ventrolateral prefrontal cortex* (RVLPFC). Furthermore, Lieberman discusses findings that show quite clearly that engaging in one form of self-control (e.g. financial) may unintentionally induce self-control in other domains (e.g. emotional), and that all of these functions occur in the RVLPFC. It's this region of the brain that he therefore refers to as "the brain's braking system."

Finally, and most relevant to the topic at hand, Lieberman references a study he helped conduct wherein participants were shown pictures of people exhibiting emotionally expressive faces and asked to either choose an emotional word to describe it (affect labeling), a gender-appropriate word to describe it (gender labeling) or simply look at the picture. For example, each participant might be shown an image of a smiling woman and asked to label it "happy" (affect labeling), "female" (gender labeling), or not label it at all. He writes:

> What we found is that a single region of the brain, RVLP-FC, was more active during affect labeling compared to gender labeling …. In other words, putting feelings into words turns on the brain's braking system. Indeed, we also found evidence that affect labeling led to self-control effects. When people engaged in affect labeling, RVLPFC activity increased, but activity throughout the limbic system in general and in the amygdala in particular, diminished. Putting feelings into words diminished participant's emotional responses to emotional pictures even though putting feelings into words involves attending to the emotional aspects of the pictures.[63]

This is the crux of "name it to tame it." Talking about an emotional response can actually diminish the intensity of the response. In effect, Lieberman argues that putting feelings into words is a highly effective form of "emotional regulation." This is good news for ourselves and those we lead. We can engage the brain's braking system and ward off an unwanted emotional response just by labeling the emotion and how it is affecting us. This is one of the reasons why the coach approach to leadership is so powerful.

Here are two strategies you can use for yourself and those you lead to leverage this powerful emotional regulation strategy:

1. **Write it down.** When you can articulate what you are feeling, you'll calm down and be in a better position to ask for what you need to move forward. Keep a journal and pen with you (or keep a notebook

app on your phone or computer) so that you're never left empty-handed when the opportunity to write presents itself.

2. **Talk to someone.** Your manager, a coach, a colleague or a friend. Engaging your thinking brain and then putting those thoughts or feelings into words can have a profound effect on regulating your emotional responses. Choose a good listener who really listens and will ask questions that challenge your assumptions and help you move forward.

Now we both understand the importance of Mom's advice to "Use your words!" Simply acknowledging our emotions can be enough to change them. And that's good news—not just for our mothers, but also for our coworkers, our reputation and our effectiveness as leaders.

6

COUNT TO
TEN

Not long ago, I was dealing with a representative of some unionized employees. Being external to the organization, the rep implied some things that I strongly felt were not true of our culture, leadership practices and employee relations. Some of the employees being represented were in the room for the discussion, and I was keenly aware that their eyes were on me for my reaction to these implications. I felt my heart pound, my chest tighten, the blood rush to my head, and my shoulders stiffen. Threat response! Amygdala hijack!

Heading into this meeting, I had anticipated this might happen because I had seen this person in action in previous meetings, and I was concerned they might try to stir an emotional response to evoke a reaction in management that would be seen as unfavourable by the employees present. When I noticed the physiological responses that were happening within my body as a result of the rep's words, I was able to catch myself before I said something that would have made things worse. Instead, I was able stay calm and help the group facilitate finding a solution.

I must admit, keeping emotions in check when upset is a leadership quality I admire in others. I've seen some leaders be too cool, which comes off as emotionless, and that doesn't work either. Showing just enough emotion so that others understand your feelings and conviction is important, all while not appearing to be losing your cool or having a meltdown. My personal leadership philosophy is rooted in the im-

portance of finding the delicate balance of leading with both heart and backbone in all situations, and most importantly in emotionally-charged situations.

Amygdala Hijack

The amygdala is essential to your ability to experience a variety of emotions, including threats in life and at work.

If information sent from your senses to your brain suggests a threat, the amygdala can kick in and initiate a response before that information is sent to the PFC—the thinking brain. The brain is wired this way so that our body can respond to threat without needing to contemplate a course of action. For example, when you hear a branch of a tree crack above you while walking, you are covering your head and getting out of that spot before you even have time to consider your options. It's an important primal instinct. That's a situation where giving your thinking brain time to think wouldn't be a smart choice. Thanks to our negativity bias, this instinctive reaction is incredibly common. Unfortunately, it is not always warranted in a world free from many of the dangers our prehistoric ancestors must have faced.

An "amygdala hijack," a term coined by psychologist and author Daniel Goleman, occurs when our emotional brain instructs our response even though the situation would be better served by a reaction from our thinking brain.

An amygdala hijack is essentially an irrational, emotional reaction—or overreaction—to a stimulus or event. It happens when the amygdala initiates the release of a rush of stress hormones before the prefrontal lobes have a chance to regulate executive function and mediate the reaction.[64] They're so common that they've even given rise to the adoption of a similar term—the amygdala hangover—to describe the regret you feel over your inappropriate responses, when you shake your head and ask yourself, "Why did I do (or say) that?"

While the fight-or-flight amygdala reflex has undoubtedly been largely responsible for the survival of the human race, our brains have not evolved to our present environment where we're less likely to come across sabre-toothed tigers than we are to encounter disengaged employees, disrespectful customers or boundary-pushing colleagues. Each of these encounters, however, still has the potential to trigger an amygdala hijack because they are, in effect, threatening our well-being on a level more representative of today's challenges regarding survival. Connecting back with the learning from Lessons 1-3, our brains are even more likely to experience an amygdala hijack when we are lacking sleep, activity, and nutrition.

If a situation is best served by rational thought and decision-making, yet our emotional brain dictates our reaction before the prefrontal cortex has a chance to get involved, things often go awry. The secret to avoiding an amygdala hijack and all the chaos that ensues can be found in Mom's time-tested advice: "Count to 10." This allows time for our thinking brain to kick in and address the issue more logically.

The quote by neurologist, psychiatrist and noted Holocaust survivor Viktor Frankl says it best: "Between stimulus and response there is a space. In that space is our power to choose our response. In our response lies our growth and our freedom."[65]

Preventing Overreactions in the Workplace

Executive functions of the prefrontal cortex are increasingly needed to succeed in the workplace. The neurocognitive components of the PFC, including the concepts of attention, memory and insight, are significant in terms of both individual and organizational leadership. They are also the precise functions that get bypassed in an amygdala hijack because our brain goes into survival mode rather than thinking mode.

The work environment is a place of many negative emotions as a result of stress, ineffective leadership, and disengaged employees. Whether we're dealing with unruly customers, inconsiderate coworkers or an inattentive boss, the ability to control emotions and keep our composure can be difficult.

Overreacting in the workplace, such as we often do during an amygdala hijack, is hard on the reputation and can be tough to overcome. It's therefore critical to prevent hijacks whenever possible, especially if you're the leader; maintaining a work environment free from perceived threats will improve the performance of those you lead. Though it's a skill that needs to be learned and practised, you can reduce your likelihood of experiencing an amygdala hijack by changing the way your brain responds to emotional triggers—and by taking responsibility for the gap between stimulus and response.

For any real growth to occur, you'll need to start taking notice of the sequence of events that leads to an amygdala hijack. Identify the triggers and then determine a more appropriate response to use next time. Your amygdala learns from past experiences, so you really can teach it to react differently in a similar situation in the future.

Despite your best of intentions to "name it to tame it," and Mom's advice to "Count to 10," hijacks and inappropriate responses will happen. When they do, there's nothing wrong with taking a "timeout" and thinking about what happened. You're human; you're emotional. But you're also capable of training your emotions to best serve yourself and those you lead. While you're giving yourself a timeout to reflect on your reaction, keep in mind the following:

10 tips for Regaining (or Keeping) Your Composure

1. **Give yourself time to think** about the situation before responding.

2. **Notice your reactions.** What are your assumptions? Approach others with an open mind.

3. **Look at things from a 30,000-foot perspective.** Pick your battles, and don't sweat the small stuff. Ask yourself, "Does it really matter?" In six months, one year, or five years, will this situation make a difference?

4. **Ask yourself what it was about the event or situation that upset you.** Would it have upset other people to the same degree that it upset you?

5. **Practise curiosity.** Being genuinely curious about the perspectives of others shifts the issue from the emotional brain to the thinking brain, and enables capacity for empathy.

6. **Evaluate how you react under pressure.** The ability to show grace under pressure is a widely-sought skill.

7. **Practise active listening.** When you feel a rush of the stress hormones cortisol and adrenaline, hold onto your thoughts and listen to what the other person is saying to try to understand their perspective. This will give you time to think, and it will help calm the other person as well.

8. **Take responsibility for your words and actions.** Be honest and act with good intention.

9. **Take responsibility for your own brain health.** Get plenty of sleep, exercise, and eat well. A lack of self-care may have contributed to your reaction.

10. **Breathe.** Inhale for ten seconds, hold for five seconds, and exhale for ten seconds. Repeat until calm.

We all experience challenging emotions. What defines us is how we respond to them. An honest self-evaluation will help you discern what you need to work on. Above all though, remember the advice you knew all along: "Count to 10." Your mother was suggesting you take time for your thinking brain to process whatever stimulus was about to set you off, so that you could respond rationally rather than emotionally.

NOTES FOR PART III

I want to remember:

_____

I want to stop:

_____

I want to start:

_____

The biggest thing preventing me from taking action is:

_____

I plan to overcome this by:

_____

Two things I will do are:

   1. _____

   2. _____

The day I will start is:

_____

PART IV

THE SOCIAL BRAIN

In Part I, you were introduced to the emotional brain and the thinking brain. Here in Part IV, we're going to explore another concept: the social brain. We will review the research pertaining to our need for social acceptance and discover the myriad ways that our brains react to social stimuli.

Our need to fit in is rooted in our intuitive knowledge that we are stronger together than alone. Although we label our modern groups as "teams" and "communities," groups of individuals who banded together were traditionally called "tribes." Our tribal instincts know that we must align with others to form a network that will serve us in the face of danger. The book *Tribal Leadership*, by Dave Logan, John King and Halee Fischer-Wright, does a good job of outlining how individuals interact and succeed together as tribes.[66]

Luckily, the same wiring that makes us want to be with each other has evolved to allow us to behave and react appropriately, limiting our self-interested compulsions for the greater good. You'll learn in Part IV how Mom's advice to "Be nice!" is not only good for other people; it's also good for your own mind and body.

Despite the fact that people have a fundamental need to feel accepted and to make a difference, organizations have become less personal due to rapid growth, workplace virtualization, competitive pressures and increasingly impersonal communication tools. Today's leaders often talk more about numbers and technology than they do about people and relationships. Consequently, as organizations grow, relationships tend to weaken. It's the quality of the relationships, however, that is most important when it comes to achieving greatness.

The social brain has direct relevance to your role as a leader. Research has shown, for example, that social rewards are often more important than money in terms of an individual's happiness.[67] Case in point, I have interviewed numerous people who were willing to leave their higher-paying jobs for the job for which I was interviewing. What was often driving them away from their current company was "the people," feeling like they didn't fit in, or lack of appreciation. We all know that money doesn't buy happiness; it doesn't buy job satisfaction or engagement either.

Let's dive into some of the ways our desire for social acceptance can influence the performance and engagement of ourselves and those we lead based on things our mothers said to us.

7

DON'T LEAVE ANYONE OUT

When I was doing my master's, one of my instructors asked us to write down a word that represented the one thing in the world we wanted most. I thought and thought, but only one word came to mind and I was sure it was silly. It was almost unnerving to write it down, but I did write it and then hastily sealed it up in the envelope provided. Fast-forward several years, and I finally understand what I was feeling when I arrived at that word. The word was acceptance.

It makes sense now because I understand the social underpinnings of our tribal instincts to align ourselves with people who accept us, who we feel can help us, who have our back, or who could be of value. We often do this subconsciously. Nowhere do I feel more accepted than I do with my family. I'm very blessed and grateful that I don't have to work that hard to be accepted by them. Thankfully, they are stuck with me. And thankfully, I'm stuck with them. Acceptance and loyalty are givens among most families, which makes our families the most precious group in our lives.

Beyond family, we need to work a little harder to figure out whom we want to align with to make us stronger. I can see a pattern in those I've chosen to align myself with. Starting in elementary school through to my graduate studies and in the workplace, I've always aligned myself with the smartest people in the group. Not surprisingly, this group represents my closest friends to this day.

I can clearly see how these groups have made me stronger. On the other hand, there have been many times when I didn't feel part of a group. Sometimes it didn't matter. But sometimes it did; and it hurt to not feel accepted. Now, with an understanding of neuroscience and the social brain, I understand why I felt this way, and I understand how everyone is really working in concert to build their own network (tribe). And it's not uncommon—though usually without intention—for them to leave people out while doing so. When it comes to leadership, having everyone feel part of the group is essential.

In-group and Out-group Bias

In the summer of 1954, social psychologists Muzafer and Carolyn Sherif, along with a team of researchers, conducted a famous experiment in Robber's Cave State Park in Oklahoma. Known as the Robber's Cave Study,[68] the experiment saw two dozen 12-year-old boys assigned to one of two groups of campers; at first each group was oblivious to the other's existence. Researchers encouraged each group to bond internally through the pursuit of common goals over the first week of the camp, and then eventually brought the two groups together and pitted them against each other in a series of contests. That's when relationships went sideways.

What started as name-calling and good-natured "razzing" quickly escalated into what could most accurately be described as dislike between the two groups. One group went so far as to burn the other group's flag, and each group refused to eat in the same mess hall as the other.[69]

For the next phase of the experiment, the groups were allowed opportunities to come together for social activities like movie nights and fireworks displays, with the hypothesis that perhaps that would lessen tensions between the groups. Instead, however, no discernible change was noticed in the negative opinions of each group toward the other.

Finally, researchers created a series of tasks in which the groups were forced to work together, such as remedying the staged vandalism of the camp's water supply, a joint decision on which movie to watch and the freeing of a food truck that was evidently stuck in a rut. These tasks, it turned out, did much to bring the groups together and eliminate the hatred and distrust. At the end of camp, most of the boys agreed that they wanted to ride home from camp on the same bus, and one boy even suggested that the five dollars won by his group in one of the earlier contests be used to buy malts for all the boys in both groups.

Though the Robber's Cave Study has not been without its criticisms, what is clear is that it demonstrates a phenomenon known as *in-group bias*, sometimes referred to as "in-group" and "out-group" thinking. David Rock, director of the Neuroleadership Institute, referred to it as "in-group preference" and "out-group bias" when he wrote:

> The phenomena known as 'in-group preference' and 'out-group bias' refer to the consistent finding that people feel greater trust and empathy toward people who are similar to themselves and are part of their same social circles, and greater distrust and reduced empathy toward those who are perceived as dissimilar and members of other social groups.[70]

"A sense of relatedness is what you get when you feel you belong to the group, when you feel part of a cohesive team," wrote Rock in his 2009 book, *Your Brain at Work*. "A feeling of relatedness is a primary reward for the brain, and an absence of relatedness generates a primary threat."[71]

Because of our survival instincts and desire to be part of a tribe where we are stronger as a collective, it's very important for the brain to determine if someone is a friend (in-group) or a foe (out-group). There is significant research, other than the Robber's Cave Study, that shows the benefits of in-group cohesion and the destructiveness of out-group hostility for organizations, communities, nations and races. We tend to like and accept people whom we consider to be part of our group (our tribe), while hostility is much more easily triggered toward those we view as outside of our group. The consequences of low relatedness—or out-group thinking—are hostility, silo thinking and Schadenfreude (taking pleasure from the pain of others).

When people feel in-group with each other, they get along and work together more effectively. They feel more acceptance, less stress and greater empathy.[72] Without empathy, groups will lack understanding and trust, and the ability to collaborate will be minimal.

The concept of in-group bias was one of the biggest "Aha!" moments of my neuroleadership studies. Personally, I feel like I'm hard-wired to walk into a room and immediately recognize all the ways I'm different, or out-group from the other people there. My sister, on the other hand, is always talking about the great new friends she meets everywhere she goes. She has a profound ability to recognize the similarities between herself and others, or to see all the ways she's in-group with the people she meets. I've always admired that ability and am continually challenging myself to be more cognizant of the things I have in common with others.

Unfortunately, because of negativity bias, you're more likely to be similar to me than you are to my sister. For most people, the brain's default is to perceive a stranger as an enemy. Given that propensity to expect a threat, we need to train our brains to see the similarities between ourselves and others in order to move them from out-group to in-group, particularly at work where collaboration is essential. In other words, we need to increase the "relatedness" we feel between ourselves and others—and create the conditions for our team members to do the same.

How we decide who's in our group and who isn't can be based on just about anything. Do they work in the same department? Do they cheer for the same sports team? Maybe they're fans of the same TV show. If you can find just a few things in common with the people around you, it's enough to move your perspective of someone from out-group to in-group.

In order to increase empathy, you need to search for common traits between yourself and the people around you. Like the employee who is often late for work because of getting children off to school; perhaps as a parent you've been in their shoes. Or perhaps the employee who would obviously rather be anywhere but there serving customers is having difficulties at home; you've also experienced rough days at home and work, and you probably know how they feel. All of these commonalities increase the chances of in-group thinking, acceptance and empathy.

At the end of the day, we're all human. The degrees of separation between us are actually quite small, and we all want primarily the same things. Even those who seem to thrive on being different or standing out still want to belong and to be accepted by their tribe. Think about the people who often dress in "goth" style in high school, usually wearing dramatic makeup and dark clothes to showcase their individuality and show that they're not part of the main group. However, who do they spend their time with? That's right—other people who like to dress and act just like them. Though they strive to be different, they're careful not to tread too far beyond the accepted norms of their own group.

In-group and out-group thinking is more prevalent than you might think. Over the next few days, pay attention to how many times you hear language such as "we" and "they" (or "us" and "them"). Whether your team is complaining about the folks at head office (them), or your colleague is justifying why that's the way it's done in this department (we)—when you hear these specific word references, it is evidence of in-group and out-group thinking. Next time you find yourself feeling out-group, challenge yourself to see things from the others' perspective, and challenge yourself to find at least two things in common with them.

In-group Bias and Collaboration

Traditional command-and-control leadership styles that were prevalent in the industrial era when people were paid to perform routine tasks are nowhere near as effective in today's knowledge-based working environments. The study of neuroscience has offered significant insight into why those command-and-control leadership styles trigger threat responses in workers and do not serve the social and emotional needs of others. In tandem with this, the complexity of business has increased significantly because of increased global competition and virtualization. Leaders need to be able to untap the potential of those they lead across distant and diverse boundaries to leverage the benefits of collaborative thinking.

Change is constant in today's marketplace, and so is the necessity to collaborate in order to move forward. Research has shown that motivation and performance go up in relation to increases in social connections to other people or groups.[73] If people need to work together to collaborate, the ability to foster relatedness amongst the group is an essential leadership competency.

Given the importance of relatedness, and the implications on organizational cohesiveness and collaboration, it is paramount that, as a leader, you prioritize a culture of in-group thinking for all team members. That starts with simply being aware of in-group bias and how in-group and out-group dynamics may be affecting your group. What are you seeing and what aren't you seeing? How many interpersonal conflicts could be avoided by encouraging your team to see each other as on the same side? How much more productive would your collaboration efforts be if you could remove any vestiges of out-group thinking?

When collaboration goes well, group members greatly benefit from the social connection with others in addition to the shared reward of group success. But the benefits of relatedness go far beyond being happy in your job. Research shows that mortality rates are lower for people who feel workplace support,[74] and those with strong social networks increase their chances of survival by 50% over those with weak social networks.[75]

Working in collaboration with others, however, is not easy terrain to navigate. As Rock writes, "the social world is the source of tremendous conflict, and many people never master its seemingly chaotic rules."[76]

Despite the social benefits of collaboration and its growing necessity in today's workplaces, our natural inclination is to not socialize outside of our groups. As discussed, we are, in fact, hard-wired to perceive others as foes (see negativity bias, Lesson 4), which tends to make collaboration difficult. It's one thing, of course, to know that in-group and out-group thinking is as prevalent as it is—even within your own organization. It's another thing entirely to know what to do about it.

Understanding our own internal drive to survive and align with people or groups that will support this can help us understand why we do what we do. Groups and tribal behaviour are part of life, and it's unrealistic to think that everyone can be part of a single group. But in the case where you lead a team, department or organization, fostering in-group thinking within your group will strengthen trust, empathy and overall performance.

Here are a few ways you can help foster productive collaboration within your organization:

1. **Foster in-group thinking and acceptance of all.** You can increase relatedness between coworkers, branches or divisions through the organization of group activities that transcend organizational divides. Encourage expressions of gratitude, the sharing of broader organizational goals and the implementation of team-building activities that aim to

identify likenesses between collaborative partners.

2. **Foster respectful disagreement and ensure that all voices are heard.**
    Dissenters are often treated poorly by people subscribing to the majority
    opinion; that treatment can sometimes go as far as shaming or shunning.
    Interestingly, dissenters sometimes care *most* about the group. Like cor-
    porate whistle-blowers who are vilified as enemies of the corporation,
    dissenters often dissent precisely because they feel the majority opinion
    or group actions violate the group's broader mandate or fail to serve its
    long-term interests. As leader, you must create a culture in which dis-
    agreement is not just acceptable, but encouraged. Hold back on being
    first to offer your perspective so that you can hear others out, and recruit
    people who do not always agree with your perspective.

3. **Foster both individual and team accountability**. Your challenge is to
    break down the barriers to contribution and make sure that everyone
    in the group is needed. You want to minimize or eliminate those who
    are not contributing, and are instead coasting on the work of others.
    You must ensure each team member knows his or her responsibilities,
    and you must develop a system for tracking progress and success. As
    the saying goes, "What gets measured gets done."

4. **Anticipate—and plan for—possible threat and reward responses.**
    Remember the SCARF model (David Rock), and be aware of when
    group members may feel threatened by status, certainty, autonomy, re-
    latedness or fairness.

Breaking into a new group that one perceives to be united by a common bond
can be very hard. Each member of your organization is likely to see him or
herself as out-group with at least some of the other members. We all know what
it feels like to be left out. What we may not realize is just how bad it is for us
physically as well as emotionally. Being rejected increases inflammation in the
body[77] and has also been shown to cause mental health issues.[78] As a leader, it's
your job to help employees recognize their commonalities to ensure that they
can collaborate productively.

All of which is just a fancier take on when our mothers said: "Don't leave anyone out."

8

BE
NICE

The use of sarcasm is a challenging dynamic to navigate and manage in the workplace. Though it's usually camouflaged as humour, sarcasm is often a way for passive aggressive people to be critical or express their opinion. These people genuinely think they are smart and funny, but their approach can cause emotional anguish in others and erode relationships. On the other hand, joking or teasing can be a healthy part of a workplace culture when there is enough trust in place for people to feel secure that the comments aren't intended to chip away at their credibility or confidence.

As a leader, I have seen how sarcasm can leave people feeling defensive and hurt, and I've been careful to manage this kind of communication style and lead by example.

This isn't just a dynamic that I've kept an eye on at work. Every time my son Austin left for a hockey trip when he was growing up, I would say, "Have fun, keep your head up, and keep sarcasm to a minimum." It became a joke, but he understood the intent of my message. Reflecting back on that ongoing thread between us, like all mothers, I intuitively knew that it was important to be nice, but I didn't understand the breadth of my motherly wisdom until I studied the neuroscience of the social needs of our brain.

Social Pain

A study published in the Journal of Applied Psychology provides evidence to support the dark side of sarcasm. Researchers found that experiencing rude behaviour like sarcasm from a coworker evokes a threat response in the brain that increases mental fatigue and reduces a person's ability to manage their emotions. As a result of the cognitive stress that is caused, researchers found that the recipients of the poor behaviour usually pass it on to someone else at some point that day.[79] Unfortunately, rudeness is contagious and this kind of ripple effect increases stress and disengagement within the workplace.

Neuroscientist Matthew Lieberman has done research that shows social pain can be perceived just as much as physical pain. His book, *Social,*[80] is an excellent read to garner further insight on this topic. Through research with Naomi Eisenberger, Lieberman discovered that physical pain and social rejection are processed by the brain in the same way. That is to say, the areas of the brain that are triggered by physical pain are the exact same areas that are activated when people feel rejected. As far as the brain is concerned, a broken heart and a broken arm are the same thing.[81]

Perhaps it shouldn't come as such a surprise, then, that researchers have found that the same acetaminophen (Tylenol) that we take to numb physical pain also numbs social pain.[82] I'm certainly not advocating acetaminophen to numb a broken heart, but it definitely provides compelling evidence of Lieberman and Eisenberger's observations.

We wouldn't go around kicking people or otherwise causing them physical pain, nor would we condone this kind of behaviour in our workplace. But how often do we or those we lead say or do things that cause feelings of exclusion or hurt feelings and consequently *social* pain? It probably happens more than we'd like to admit. This connects back to Mom's last lesson of not leaving anyone out and the neurological implications of in-group and out-group behaviour and thinking.

Empathy Fuels Connection

Not only does social pain light up the same area of the brain as physical pain, but that part of the brain is also activated when we see someone else in pain.[83]

This is known as empathy, which is the ability to understand what others are experiencing. Empathy is an important interpersonal skill of emotionally intelligent leaders because it fuels connection and compassion because people feel understood and accepted.[84] Empathy is different from sympathy. Sympathy is feeling badly for someone; empathy is understanding how someone feels. An example of sympathy might be saying something like, "I am sorry that you failed your test." On the other hand, empathy in this situation would sound like, "I can understand your disappointment."

Caring for Others is Good For You

It turns out that being nice isn't only good for others; it's good for you too. A study led by Barbara Fredrickson, a professor at the University of North Carolina, suggests that being kind to others has been traced to activity of a specific nerve system in the body called the vagus nerve. The vagus nerve not only regulates immune response and glucose; it is also connected to tuning our hearing to human speech, eye contact, and how we regulate our emotional expressions. The vagus nerve is like a highway that connects your body and your brain. Fredrickson said that the biggest finding from the study was evidence to support that increasing the amount of positive emotion in people's life can activate the vagus nerve which positively impacts physical health. She suggests that this helps explain "how our emotional and social experience affects our physical health."[85]

On top of caring for others, you can also stimulate the vagus nerve through yoga, meditation, socializing, deep breathing, laughter, exercise, and getting out in the sun.[86]

Be Grateful

Being nice includes showing gratitude to others. Great news! This nice gesture is also good for your brain. The Greater Good Science Center at the University of California has found that gratitude is connected to your brain's reward system, and that when we express our gratitude to others we experience positive physical, social and psychological benefits. Conveying our appreciation floods the brain with positive chemicals that specifically work to increase our connectedness with others. Expressing gratitude is an easy way to increase relatedness between you and those you lead. In a 2003 study, "scientists saw the benefits of simply writing down what you're grateful for. After 10 weeks, people who kept a gratitude journal were more optimistic, had fewer physical ailments and exercised more than people who wrote down things that annoyed them."[87]

Besides the social benefits of gratitude, studies have shown that people who regularly express gratitude experience positive emotions more often and are more empathetic, forgiving, helpful and supportive than those who don't.[88]

Simple ideas to leverage the cognitive and leadership benefits of being nice:

1. Help others – caring for others activates the vagus nerve, which is good for your mind and your body.

2. Express gratitude – write thank you notes, record your thoughts in a gratitude journal, or make a daily point of thanking someone.

3. Minimize behaviour that causes social pain like exclusion and sarcasm. Practise empathy over sympathy. Use phrases like, "I understand," or "I can relate."

For the emotional regulation and well-being of ourselves and those we lead, we need to remember our mothers' wise words, "Be nice!"

9

KEET IT TO
YOURSELF

Have you ever worked with one of those people whose response to a simple, "How are you?" could set the tone for your whole day? I have, and it was exhausting. Their response could range from a "Great!" to an eye roll, or to a grunt. Their unpredictability made me hold my breath awaiting their response. When they were in a good mood, my threat responses were not activated and I'd breathe out in relief, but any hint of the opposite could make my brain panic a little bit, trying to determine how to best navigate around them throughout my day. Emotions are contagious—some more so than others—and some personalities are more in-clined than others to force their moods onto others. I can't think of a time where someone else's bad mood was a welcome addition to my morning.

As a naturally empathetic person, I am careful not to intentionally say things that hurt others. Nonetheless, I have had days when the pressure got to me, and the people around me were impacted by my less than cheerful mood. Through my studies of the social brain, I've learned the importance of making sure my negative thoughts and emotions don't spread to others.

Emotions are Contagious

The term emotional contagion means that emotions are contagious, and that is something our mothers may have been well aware of when they told us, "Keep it to yourself," or "If you don't have anything nice to say, then don't say anything at all." The fact that emotions are contagious is more important than you might realize in terms of leading self and others.

Emotionally-intelligent leaders understand that their moods have a significant impact on workplace culture and performance. If you are able to positively and enthusiastically influence the emotions of the people around you, performance will soar. This is what's referred to as *resonance*. Conversely, if your emotions affect the people around you negatively, it creates feelings of acrimony, anxiousness and discontent—known as *dissonance*.[89]

Optimistic moods have been shown to increase cooperation, fairness and performance. On the other hand, negative emotions—such as anger and anxiety—cause stress and disrupt our thinking.[90] This, unsurprisingly, has a direct impact on an organization's bottom line. One study found that management teams that were more positive and worked cooperatively achieved better overall financial results.[91]

The relationship between emotional intelligence and leadership was explored in great depth by authors Daniel Goleman, Richard E. Boyatzis and Annie McKee in their book, *Primal Leadership: Learning to Lead with Emotional Intelligence*. Among many other fascinating revelations, the authors revealed that it's not only what leaders say that matters; it's what they do and how they do it.

Goleman, Boyatzis and McKee cite studies that show that, in group situations, people watch leaders more than anyone else, looking to see the leaders' responses and often modeling them. The leader, therefore, is largely responsible for establishing the emotional climate of the group. Other studies have shown that up to 70% of employees trace their organization's emotional climate back to the leader.[92] How the boss shows up sets the stage for the emotional climate of the entire workplace. Your ability to manage your emotions, therefore, has a significant impact on your organization's success.

We've all witnessed a grumpy or otherwise negative leader whose negativity spreads throughout the workplace. This is very often at the root of so-called toxic environments. On the other hand, I'm sure you can also recall a leader whose positivity created an environment of optimism—an environment that inspired the best out of workers.

As a leader, your energy can create a dramatic ripple effect throughout your entire organization. Experiments on emotional contagion have shown that if strangers sit in silence facing each other, the person who is most emotionally easy to read will influence the mood of the other.[93] Take three people and sit them in a room together. If two of them are smiling and happy, what happens to the other? He or she becomes happy, too.

A study from Yale University found not only that moods impact workplace performance, but also that cheerfulness and warmth spread more easily than sadness or depression. The most contagious emotional response, it turns out, is laughter, which tends to spark a positive emotional hijack in the people surrounding it. Laughter, therefore, is a great indicator of a positive environment in which hearts and minds are fully engaged, and in which workers have a strong positive connection to their workplace.

With research showing that an employee's positivity toward his or her workplace is a strong predictor of satisfaction and is therefore directly linked to retention, it's no wonder emotional intelligence is a skill increasingly sought after for leadership positions. Emotionally-intelligent leaders are better able to control how their emotions affect the people around them, which in turn leads to increased cooperation, engagement and performance.

Unfortunately, emotional contagion also happens in reverse, which can have far-reaching consequences and a lasting impact. Harvard Business Review noted that "we often perceive even greater judgment and negativity than actually exists. And these effects can last for 26 hours or more, imprinting the interaction on our memories and magnifying the impact it has on our future behavior. Cortisol functions like a sustained-release tablet—the more we ruminate about our fear, the longer the impact."[94]

A study by former Yale professor Dr. Sigal Barscade explored the effects of emotional contagion on group decisions and dynamics. Dr. Barscade divided business school students into several groups and asked them to role-play a department head advocating for an employee's merit-based pay increase while balancing that against a limited budget for the entire "company." To make things interesting, in each group she planted an actor who displayed one of four emotional states: cheerful enthusiasm, serene warmth, hostile irritability or depressed sluggishness. Not only did Barscade find that the groups infiltrated by a cheerful actor ended the experiment in a decidedly more cheerful mood, but she also found that those groups cooperated better, experienced less conflict and self-assessed their performance higher than the other groups. Surprisingly, they also allocated their money in a more equitable manner, even though they had no inkling that their decisions had been influenced by mood.[95]

As a leader, it is vitally important that you understand both the positive and negative implications of emotional contagion. While every member of a group adds to the emotional mix, the leader adds the most because it's the leader to whom other group members look for direction. When you set a positive emotional tone in your workplace, that positivity and corresponding productivity will transfer to the entire group. Show up in a foul mood and you risk devastating effects on morale throughout your entire team.

Containing the Grumpiness

Let's face it, most of us have times when we don't feel as positive as we would like for one reason or another. If you're having one of those days, here are some ideas to keep your negativity from becoming someone else's problem:

1. **Notice your mood.** Sounds simple, but it's not practised often enough. It's unlikely that your intention would be to negatively impact others. If you take time to notice how you are feeling (self-awareness), you can keep it to yourself if it's only going to take the air out of the room for others.

2. **Be aware of the emotions your body language is portraying.** Are you crossing your arms? What facial expressions are you offering? What's the tone in your voice?

3. **If practical, keep your distance from people who tend to get under your skin when you are cranky.** It's best not to test your resolve when you're not feeling at your best.

4. **Remember Mom's 6th lesson: Count to 10.** Is this the best time to respond? Before you respond to an email or voice message that has irritated you, count to 10. Better yet, leave it overnight.

5. **Take a timeout.** Go for a walk or redirect your attention to something else.

6. **Are you h-angry (hungry and therefore angry)?** If so, fuel your body and mind.

7. **Find your happy place.** (Kidding, but not really kidding.) Is it music, or a conversation with a friend or colleague? Pursue that which helps you see that "it's not the end of the world." Silly animal videos on the Internet, for example, usually get a smile out of even the crankiest of persons. In all seriousness, you need to take responsibility for your own grumpiness and try to shake it—or at least contain it—so it doesn't spread to others.

Consider your ripple effect. We either give life or suck the life out of people. If you know that you're in a bad mood, you have the power to either spread your negativity or keep it to yourself so it doesn't become infectious.

Conversely, you need to be aware of how the emotions of the people in your workplace are affecting *you*. If someone is sucking the life out of you, don't just sit idly by and let it happen, as that can quickly lead to a toxic environment that impacts not only the mood, but also the quality of work delivered by everyone in that workplace.

A demanding workplace requires an empathetic and supportive leader who can manage the creative tension associated with performance expectations and engagement. That doesn't mean you have to be overly nice or obsequious. You just need to remember Mom's advice when you are in a bad mood: "Keep it to yourself."

NOTES FOR PART IV

I want to remember:

_____

I want to stop:

_____

I want to start:

_____

The biggest thing preventing me from taking action is:

_____

I plan to overcome this by:

_____

Two things I will do are:

1. _____

2. _____

The day I will start is:

_____

PART V

FOCUS

May I have your attention?

The ability to pay attention is essential, both for our individual and our organizational success, yet we've never before experienced an age with so many distractions vying for our attention. From emails, to social media notifications, to advertisements, it seems more difficult than ever to focus these days. Despite all these distractions, you still need to pay attention to what matters: your deadlines, your relationships, your personal health and well-being … at the very least, you need to pay attention while driving!

The average person looks at their phone 47 times a day and experiences an interruption every three minutes.[96] Once an interruption has occurred, research says it takes anywhere from 5-23 minutes to return to the original task.[97] Yikes! At this rate, we're falling behind more and more every hour.

Besides technological distractions, we're also locked in a fierce battle for attention with our own minds. One study of over 650,000 real-time responses via text message from more than 15,000 people found that people's minds wander nearly half of the day (47%).[98] Unfortunately, during these periods of mind-wandering, people report being less happy than when they are in the present moment.

What are you thinking about when your mind wanders? Often, it's worry. With information being so prevalent, we are aware of the dangers near and far, from disease, terrorism and credit card fraud to identity theft, climate change and gluten. We are constantly being bombarded with information about potential threats to ourselves and our loved ones, and our negativity bias is in overdrive scanning for danger. This bombardment triggers the fight-or-flight response in our emotional brain, and our response is generally negative.

Believe it or not, the art of paying attention can be mastered through practise— and it's particularly important to do just that, because what you pay attention to will determine how you will build and strengthen your brain tissue. Your neurons wire in response to what you focus on; if your brain is constantly scattered or you focus on the negative, that will become your reality. If you focus instead on what is most important, and what is possible and achievable, then your reality will be a much happier place.

Part V explores the importance of focus in terms of personal and organizational leadership. And it all starts with realizing the truth behind the things your mother told you a long time ago about paying attention.

10

TURN IT
DOWN

My mom often used to tell us to turn the music down in the car, or to keep our voices down so she could think. At the time, I didn't really understand what she was talking about. It wasn't until post-secondary that I discovered how challenging it was to focus on my studies amidst distractions. In the years since, I've constantly tried to manage the noise around me so that I could focus, and I've often asked my kids to "keep it down" so I could think.

When I first started working, I used a computer with limited Internet access. Email was minimal, phones that were "smart" were nonexistent, news came from the radio, print or TV, and sending out a photocopied family Christmas letter was as close as I got to "social media." Phone, snail mail and the occasional fax were the predominant ways of communicating with someone I couldn't talk to in person. Workplace communication has rapidly become much more complicated over my 25-year career.

Today, there are so many things vying for my attention—and notifications coming at me from every direction: LinkedIn, Facebook, Twitter, Instagram, news websites, the weather, traffic and more. And that's not mentioning the texts and other instant messages from coworkers and family. Even while writing this part of the book, I've received three text messages from family and one instant message from work. With the arrival of each of these messages, I've become distracted and then needed to refocus my attention. These distractions can be troublesome when I want to really pay attention to something.

Driven to Distraction

How is one supposed to maintain focus in a world set up to distract us at every turn? As we explored in Part IV, we are hardwired to be social and to seek reward and avoid threat. Notifications are constantly telling us when there is something that may benefit or harm us, or they are advising us of the status of our social connections. Even though I understand the cognitive implications of distractions and the amount of time that is wasted checking notifications and then trying to pick up again where I left off, resisting the temptation to check these invasive notifications is challenging, especially when they are from family. To understand why this is so, we need to go back to the brain.

The chemical that the brain releases when we feel a sense of accomplishment is called dopamine; it's what makes us feel good. We feel the rush of a release of dopamine in our system when we cross something off our to-do list or achieve a goal.[99]

I'm one of those people who adds tasks that are already done to a to-do list just so I can cross them off immediately. I didn't realize why I did this until I began to understand the appeal of that dopamine injection. Similarly, every email, call and notification we receive and respond to triggers the release of a little bit of dopamine.

The bad news is that these hits of dopamine are addictive,[100] which explains why we can't resist responding to every buzz, ring or blink that comes our way. We can't help ourselves from checking notifications, even when we know logically that it is distracting us from the task on which we're trying to focus. It's textbook self-sabotaging behaviour.

Fortunately, there is also good news. With discipline, it is possible to manage these distractions. We can shut off email, turn off the sound of notifications and tune out other distractions by working in a quiet place. Also, we can train our brain to focus; that's essentially what the discipline of mindfulness is all about (coming up in Lesson 12).

The Downward Spiral of Distraction

How often does this happen to you? You're sitting at your desk concentrating on something when your mobile phone indicates you have a notification of some sort. You check it quickly, then return to the task at hand. Then a colleague asks you a "quick question." Then there's an incoming email notification … then a phone call … then an interesting bit of news on the radio that's playing in the background.

Before you know it, a half hour has gone by and you haven't done a single bit of productive work toward your original task. And then what happens? Your anxiety increases because you're further behind. The downward spiral continues until you feel overwhelmed by "things to do."

Learning to manage the noise in our environment starts with understanding that our brains can only process a few things at one time.[101] Unfortunately, there are many more than a few things going on at any given time. Even as you are reading this paragraph, millions of sensory neurons are firing. Your skin contains millions of receptors that are constantly receiving information about temperature, touch and pressure.[102] Consider everything you can feel, see, hear or smell right now. Are any parts of your body aching? Is there a distracting sound in the distance? Can you smell food? Are you hot or cold? Your brain is processing all of these things even as you try to concentrate on the task at hand.

Now add to all of that the current-day technological cacophony of devices and notifications and it's no wonder we have so much trouble focusing! If you've ever thrown up your hands and shouted, either literally or figuratively, "I just can't think!" then you know what I'm talking about. The ability to direct attention and tune out distractions has never been more critical—both to individual as well as organizational success.

The Butterfly Brain

In 2015, a study by Microsoft made headlines around the world when it announced that human attention spans are now lower than those of goldfish, falling to just eight seconds from the previous benchmark of 12 seconds in the year 2000. (Goldfish can apparently hold their attention for 9 seconds.)[103] In a complex world in which we are paid to think, this is a worrisome trend. The study also noted that more than 75% of people reach for their phones when they are bored or watching TV, and over 50 % check their phones every 30 minutes.

Josh Davis, a director of research at the Neuroleadership Institute and author of *Two Awesome Hours*, is no stranger to the effects of workplace information overload. "Our brains are designed to pick up on what's new or changing around us," he said in an interview with London's *Telegraph* newspaper. "In the digital world, things are changing and being posted every few seconds. … It's no wonder so many of us have butterfly brains."[104]

The term "butterfly brain" really caught my attention when I first happened upon it. I know that my mind flits in and out of news bits, communications, social media and even actual conversations. When I get tired or bored, my mind flutters to something new. I've even noticed an increasing preference to "text" rather than call. With text messages, I can flit in and out of conversations on my own terms, just like a butterfly. While my love for the simplicity of texting has increased, I've also noticed that I have less and less capacity and interest for lengthy conversations. Sometimes I find myself wanting to flit to the next conversation after about a text message's length of conversation.

The Goldilocks Principle

There is a well-documented relationship between pressure and performance. Generally speaking, performance improves as the pressure to perform increases, *up to a point*. Once you or your team members hit that critical tipping point a further increase in pressure corresponds with a *decrease* in performance. This is often called the "Inverted U Model," after the distinct curve that represents it when plotted on a graph. It's also known as the "performance arousal curve" and, less colourfully, the "Yerkes-Dodson Law" after the two psychologists who formulated it back in 1908.[105]

A little pressure is good but too much pressure is bad. This is what's known as the *Goldilocks Principle*. [106] Finding the point that's "just right" for yourself and those you lead is one of the most important components of personal and organizational leadership. But how do you know how much is just right?

The tipping point between pressure-improving performance and pressure-inhibiting performance, known as the "optimal arousal point," is different for everybody. It's the point at which you feel motivated rather than tired or bored—and when you feel empowered rather than stressed or out of control. Once you understand this principle, there is much you can do as a leader to maximize the performance of yourself and your team. First and foremost, knowing those you lead is paramount because only then will you start to understand where each person's optimal arousal point lies.

Your best ideas—those critical moments of insight that lead to real breakthroughs and progress—happen at that balance between a mind that's too taxed and one that's too free. If you're sitting at your desk stressing over the impending deadline and knowing that you need to come up with something fast, chances are you won't produce your best work. This is largely why only 10% of more than 6,000 workers surveyed by the Neuroleadership Institute claimed to do their best thinking at work[107]—there's simply too much pressure to perform.

In most cases, the key to moving forward with a challenge is finding a new way of thinking. Just as directed attention is critical to performance, so is a healthy dose of mind-wandering. Remember, it's all about balance.

Davis (the neuroscientist and author of *Two Awesome Hours*) advocates that mind-wandering is a precursor to insight. He cites research that shows that when the mind wanders, and it's not focusing on something negative, it gravitates toward the future. This is good news for organizations that want their leaders to be forward-thinking.[108] Most importantly, the conditions for insight depend on a resting brain, or alpha brain waves. It is imperative that leaders create environments that allow team members to find their optimal arousal point and achieve insight. Emails, meetings and an assortment of other organizational distractions create challenging conditions for a resting brain; while pressure may help narrow focus, it does little to create the conditions for insight.[109]

Once you have a basic understanding of those you lead and what makes them tick, you can start setting realistic goals that are attainable yet still ambitious. Goals that are too ambitious can lead to a distinctly demotivating sense of helplessness; if you set goals that are too easily achieved, your team will lack the motivation to perform to the best of their abilities.

Cultivating Attention

Working as we are in the knowledge era, we must have the ability to remember information. That includes both declarative memories, such as facts and information about things that have happened, and non-declarative memories, such as procedures and habits.

It's not uncommon to hear complaints in the workplace pertaining to there being "too much information" to retain. Just as you can influence your environment to bring out the best for you and your team, you can also create the conditions that contribute to the consolidation of thoughts into memory—a process known as *encoding*.

One of the most productive things you can do to foster encoding, or memory creation and retention, is to distribute learning across multiple sessions. Research has consistently shown that retention is higher when learning is broken into manageable chunks and spaced out over time compared to learning that takes place all at once.[110] If you try to learn something all at once, research shows that you won't devote as much attention to it. So rather than schedule an all-day training session, spread it out over a week in 90-minute chunks to help your team members retain more. Distributed learning leads to retention.

Strategies to Manage Workplace Distractions

Distractions in the workplace are everywhere. These derailers include everything from social media on your phone or computer, text messages, non-work emails, news feeds, unscheduled meetings, chatty coworkers, or noisy coworkers. Here are some simple things you can do to manage these distractions and give yourself a chance to focus:

1. Make a list of things that are distracting you. This will give you an opportunity to notice their frequency. Which happen most often? Which are self-inflicted? Which are caused by others?

2. In the morning (or the night before), write a list of the top three things you want to accomplish that day—and cross them off the list as you get them done.

3. Put your personal phone out of sight. If you really have a problem resisting your phone, consider closing or deleting your favourite apps, or turning off all notifications. There are apps you can set up on your phone or computer that limit your access to the Internet during certain

periods or that reward you for staying focused. This seems extreme, but I know people who have gone to this length and have had success reducing their compulsion to check their phones.

4. Ask your friends and family to limit messages to you during the work-day unless they are very important.

5. Consider a permanent out-of-office message that advises all senders that you check email only at specific, pre-determined times.

6. If you have noisy coworkers or surroundings, invest in noise-canceling headphones or listen to non-distracting music with the aid of earphones.

7. If you have coworkers who routinely interrupt your thinking for non-work related matters, ask them if they would mind if you caught up at lunch or at a scheduled time.

8. Track your time in 15-minute increments for one week, and then reflect on the data to find patterns. Notice what time of day you are generally most productive and focused, and work within that natural rhythm. Use your most productive time to tackle big projects, and your least productive time of day to reply to email.

9. Say no to unscheduled meetings, or do as Warren Buffet does, and schedule meetings no more than one day in advance. I know this is easier said than done. But it is possible to push back a little, especially to those who frequently interrupt you. Next time someone pops in on you to ask, "Can we meet for 10 minutes?" try saying, "I'd love to; let's schedule a time that works for both of us." If the offender is your boss, how about scheduling a weekly meeting to cover all your action items at once?

Can you do these things? Of course you can. They likely won't feel as gratifying as the short-term rewards of many of the distractions you've been indulging in, but the long-term benefit of being able to focus will support your well-being and performance. As our mothers warned us, we've got to "Turn it down!" What noise are you willing to turn down so that you can think?

11

YOU CAN'T DO TWO THINGS AT ONCE

Recently I was asked to speak at a national conference. In order to make it happen, I found myself running flat-out at home and at work so that I could get ahead before I went away. When I arrived at the conference, I was invited out to a baseball game the first evening with some work friends. Rather than decline, and get some much-needed sleep, I opted to go to the game and be social, ignoring the three-hour time change.

It was after midnight local time when I finally got to sleep, but that made it only 9 p.m. home time. When I woke up at 7 a.m. the next morning to prepare for a breakfast meeting, jet lag had definitely kicked in and my brain was decidedly foggy as it was 4 a.m. home time. I rushed around getting ready for the meeting while reviewing my speaking notes for my session later that day. Just before I headed out the door, I made a phone call to arrange another meeting, while I simultaneously tried on two different shoes to decide which one looked best with my suit.

I rushed down to breakfast and had a great meeting with a dynamic new CEO. After breakfast, I chatted with some work colleagues and checked in at the conference registration desk. It was only then that an old friend broke away from our hug and gasped, actually putting her hand up to her mouth in a gesture of genuine shock. I looked downward in the direction she was looking and realized with horror what had caused her dramatic reaction. I was wearing two different shoes. Not two similar shoes —two completely different shoes. Similar in height, but one was an open-toed heel and the other was a closed-toed heel.

The true irony was that I had been invited to the conference to speak on the topic of Mindful Leadership.

Busyness Syndrome

The number of people feeling as though their minds are full to capacity, especially in the business world, has reached epic proportions. I like to call it Busyness Syndrome (or BS for short!). How do you know if you suffer from Busyness Syndrome? I've come up with some tell-tale symptoms for self-diagnosis:

— You feel as though you are too busy to think and/or sleep.
— You push the "close door" button on the elevator repeatedly.
— You think debit and ATM machines take forever.
— You feel people take too long to say what they are trying to say.
— You eat lunch at your desk while checking email.
— You buy coffee rather than make it.

And in the most severe cases:

— You finish dressing or getting ready in the car (donning two mismatched shoes, perhaps?).
— You find something "productive" to do while waiting for your toast to pop up.
— You can't find the time to call your mother.

The Myth of Multitasking

Try to solve the following math problem while simultaneously crossing your arms across your chest. Ready … go:

$$6 \times 3 = ?$$

Now uncross your arms and put them by your side. Which way did you cross your arms—right over left or left over right?

This time, let's increase the complexity of the equation as well as an expectation of adapting to change. I'd like you to solve the following problem while simultaneously crossing your arms *the other way* across your chest. Go for it:

$$(15 \times 2) \div 3 = ?$$

Did you find the second problem a bit trickier than the first? What most people will do is instinctively concentrate on one part of the task over the other—either solving the problem first and then crossing the arms or vice versa. Our bodies and brains instinctively know that we can't do both at the same time.

For most of my adult life, I prided myself on my ability to multitask. Then I started learning about neuroscience and I discovered the truth: multitasking is a fallacy when it comes to cognitively-draining tasks. Sure, we can walk and drink coffee at the same time because they don't require complex cognitive function. But try maintaining a conversation while also texting, and you'll see what I mean. The thoughts you are intending to speak come out in your text message, and vice versa. Multitasking is an illusion.

When we think we're multitasking, what we're actually doing is attention-switching. The switching happens so fast that it *feels* like we're doing two things at once, but the reality is that what we're doing isn't nearly as effective as it would be if we were to focus on each task sequentially rather than simultaneously. As Albert Einstein once said, "Any man who can drive safely while kissing a pretty girl is simply not giving the kiss the attention it deserves."[111]

As outlined in the previous lesson, when we accomplish a task, our brain releases the chemical messenger dopamine into the body. We love dopamine, which is why multitasking feels so rewarding. When we believe we are doing more than one thing at a time our brain gets a strong sense of accomplishment and we're rewarded with a rush of dopamine, despite the fact that we may be making mistakes or taking more time to perform each task.

In the business world, and despite unequivocal evidence to the contrary, our society has embraced the misnomer that "effective" multitasking is one of the keys to success. How have we tricked ourselves into believing something that flies in the face of so much research? According to Sharon Salzberg, a meditation teacher and author of *Real Happiness at Work: Meditations for Accomplish-*

ment, Achievement, and Peace, it comes down to mindlessness.

"Strung out by information overload," she writes, "many of us are becoming habituated and addicted to distraction." She continues:

> 'Successful' multitasking has been shown to activate the re-ward circuit in the brain by increasing dopamine levels—the brain chemical responsible for feelings of happiness. The danger of this is that the dopamine rush feels so good that we don't notice we're making more mistakes. This is comparable to the rush you might feel while playing the slot machines in a casino. Stimulated and entertained by the flashing lights, the ringing bells, and the distracting, carnival-like atmosphere, gamblers go into a pleasure trance, addicted to the illusion of winning money when, in fact, they're going broke. It's important to be aware of how multitasking can stimulate us into mindlessness, giving the illusion of productivity while stealing our focus and harming performance.[112]

More Bad News About Multitasking

Frequent multitasking has been linked with memory impairment, increased stress levels and inability to focus on important or complicated tasks. A University of London study found that participants who multitasked during cognitive tasks experienced temporary IQ declines that were similar to what would be expected from smoking marijuana or staying up all night.[113] (A similar study commissioned by Hewlett-Packard found that the decrease in IQ caused by workplace distractions like email, phone calls and multitasking was more than *twice* as pronounced as that caused by smoking marijuana.[114]) In fact, multitasking was shown to reduce the IQ of an average adult to that of an eight-year old child. Yikes! Keep that in mind the next time you're firing off a quick email to your boss during an important meeting—you'd be just as well getting an eight-year-old child to write it for you.

With so much being thrown at us, and the burden of expectation feeling heavier and heavier, we often feel like we need to just "power through" all of our small tasks, attempting to do three or more at a time. We check email while listening to a webinar while sorting through our paperwork, thinking multitasking is the key to becoming more efficient. It's not.

The downsides of an inability to focus are well documented. One study, conducted by De Montfort University directly links the people who are heavy phone and Internet users to the odds of being forgetful and making mistakes.[115] Other studies reveal that when people are interrupted and switch their attention between tasks, they take an average of 50% longer to accomplish the task and make up to 50% more mistakes.[116]

Gloria Mark, a professor in the department of informatics at the University of California, Irvine, presented even more concerning evidence in a recent paper. After studying the online activity of 40 workers over a two-week period, the study revealed a direct correlation between shorter periods of online focus duration and a neurotic personality. And what was the median duration of online screen focus over the two-week period? *Just 40 seconds.* Stress and sleep were also shown to be inversely related with online screen focus duration, which in turn was unsurprisingly associated with lower productivity.[117] That is to say, the more stressed or sleep-deprived you are, the less likely you will be able to focus at work, and the less productive you're apt to be.

Disengaging and Re-engaging

Every time you switch tasks, your brain has to go through the complex task of disengaging the neurons that are currently working together to activate a new set of neurons to work together for the other task. Consider the number of times you check your email, text messages, or social media accounts each day—and the time and energy it takes to re-engage each time you switch your attention from one thing to another.

Daniel Levitin, a professor of behavioural neuroscience at McGill University and author of *The Organized Mind: Thinking Straight in the Age of Information Overload,* has found that attempting to multitask can lead to other unhealthy habits as well. "People eat more, and they take more caffeine. Often what you really need in that moment isn't caffeine, but just a break. If you aren't taking regular breaks every couple of hours, your brain won't benefit from that extra cup of coffee."[118]

The science is unequivocal—when you attempt to multitask, you make more mistakes, remember less, increase your stress and lower your IQ. In other words, multitasking not only makes you less efficient; it also makes you less intelligent! If you take the time to focus on your priorities, you'll increase your effectiveness significantly. If you get paid to think—which you most likely do if you hold a leadership position—you're going to be much more efficient if you knock off your tasks one at a time.

Keep Your Team's Multitasking to a Minimum

Just as you need to be conscious of your own attempts at multitasking, as a leader you also have to be conscious of the environment in which you and your team members work. It's your responsibility as leader to create a culture that fosters and supports focus. Help your team focus by adopting the following strategies:

1. Set clear priorities.

2. Block off time for specific projects or tasks.

3. Establish predetermined times for checking and responding to email.

4. Set aside uncluttered time for strategic thinking.

As the Nobel Prize-winning economist Herbert Simon once noted, "What information consumes is rather obvious: it consumes the attention of its recipients. Hence a wealth of information creates a poverty of attention."[119] Instead of trying to multitask, stay focused on one thing at a time. Rather than skimming emails, reading only headlines and subject lines and skipping through voice mails, direct your attention to, and place more importance on, the task at hand.

Then, encourage those you lead to do the same. Because like Mom said, "You can't do two things at once."

12
PAY
ATTENTION!

On many occasions, I've questioned if I would have the mental toughness and commitment to see this book through to the end. It took a lot longer than I thought, and I've contemplated giving up many times. The biggest challenge was having enough focus to make any meaningful progress when I had the time to write. And I learned that my day-to-day work does not often require me to focus on any one task for hours at a time while simultaneously leveraging my knowledge, insight and creativity. Writing a book was exhausting!

The hardest part was paying attention. Here's an example of a common scenario when I sat down to write. Just as I got writing, my attention would slip and I'd spot my phone. The next thing I knew I'd be scanning my news and social feeds. Oops, I'd quickly remind myself that I'd lost focus and put it down or out of sight. Shortly thereafter, I'd hear a conversation between my husband and son and couldn't help but listen in. Darn, lost focus again. And just when I felt like I was making progress, my brain would decide it was exhausted and I'd find myself opening the cupboard looking for something to eat—or pouring a glass of wine.

I had to dig really deep to muster up enough focus to write this book. The good news is that it got easier. I learned to manage most distractions and experienced improvement in the length of time I could pay attention to the task at hand. When my brain tired, I would often reach for my phone and check email. When I was able see that the last time I checked for notifications was an hour or two prior, I *knew that I'd achieved a level of focus that was acceptable to me. When I would see that it had only been fifteen minutes since I last checked, that was an indication that I needed to increase my focus. The irony of writing about the importance of focus while struggling to stay focused is not lost on me; it's further evidence of the challenges we face when trying to achieve our goals.*

Meditation and Mindfulness

A dictionary will tell you that to "meditate" is to focus your attention on something, and that "mindfulness" means to focus attention on the present. We all focus our attention on something in one way or another at any given time—it's a matter of what we focus our attention on that makes all the difference to our well-being.

Although "meditation and mindfulness" often have spiritual connotations, for the purpose of this book, we're going to look at them from a neuroscientific perspective. From that point of view, mindfulness meditation is quite simply the ability to direct your attention in a way that serves your well-being rather than evoke negative implications. It's the ability to gain control of thoughts that aren't serving us, and it's a powerful defence against worry, distractedness and negative thoughts. If we ruminate on what happened in the past, or catastrophize about what might happen next, the stress causes a cortisol release that isn't good for the brain, and it takes us away from focusing on the present.

Mindfulness and the Power of Focus

It's impossible to learn and remember that to which you have not paid attention. In Lesson 11, we saw that flitting back and forth between tasks does not work. Instead, we need to give each task the attention it deserves. The ability to purposefully direct attention—known in neuroscience as *cognitive control*—is essential for workplace leadership and effectiveness. When you're able to manage your attention, you can create new or stronger neuropathways in your brain.

Cognitive control takes place in the prefrontal cortex—the area of the brain in charge of abstract thinking, thought analysis and behaviour regulation.[120] Once bolstered through a bit of practise, cognitive control allows you to stay focused even in the face of disruptions or impediments. The same neural activity that enables the focused pursuit of goals also controls emotions, which is why cognitive control allows us to stay calm in times of crisis—keeping our heads while others are losing theirs.

It should come as no surprise, then, that cognitive control is a highly desirable quality of successful leaders.

In 1949, Canadian neuropsychologist Donald Hebb wrote what is now referred to as "Hebb's Law," based on the belief that your experiences become entrenched in your mind through a system of neurons.[121] That is to say, when you repeat a behaviour, the neuropathways involved in that behaviour become even stronger, and habits are formed. Once the habit is formed, your brain uses less energy because those pathways are already strengthened and the behaviour is routine.

Enter mindfulness—the training of attention often referred to as meditation. Contrary to what some believe, mindfulness is not a method of distracting your mind; rather, it's a discipline that trains you to *focus* your attention. Mindfulness helps you direct your attention in a very conscious way to help change your default tendencies. More mindfulness leads to higher emotional intelligence[122]—higher self-awareness, self-regulation, deeper motivation, better empathy and better social skills.

How Mindfulness Changes your Brain

Researchers from the University of British Columbia have found that the practice of mindfulness meditation impacts many regions of the brain, and two in particular. The first is the anterior cingulate cortex, or ACC, which is the area of the brain responsible for self-control. This is the area of the brain you rely on to focus, resist temptations and distractions, and manage your impulses.

The second area of the brain that researchers found is significantly impacted by mindfulness is the hippocampus, which is associated with emotion, memory and managing setbacks. Unfortunately, stress can have a damaging effect on the hippocampus—so much so that those who experience chronic stress have been shown to have smaller hippocampi than average, coupled with a reduced capacity for resilience.

Having the discipline to pay attention, manage emotions and resist temptation is imperative for personal and organizational leadership, and it's equally important to have the mental fortitude to be resilient in the face of change and setbacks.

Focus is Good for your Health

An 11-year study comparing 600,000 non-meditators with 2,000 meditators found significant reductions in illness and a 63% reduction in healthcare costs for those who practised meditation.[123]

Yet more research has shown that mindfulness training reduces stress hormones in the body, boosts immunity and increases focus. Other benefits include improved focus, memory, sleep and creativity, decreases in stress and anxiety, improved overall health and increased happiness. Clearly, mindfulness meditation is powerful stuff.

Mindfulness has now, thankfully, entered the mainstream. It was first introduced to the "mass market" in the 1970s by Jon Kabat-Zinn, who travelled the world teaching an eight-week course called Mindfulness-Based Stress Reduction. When participants were studied, researchers found that those who had participated in his mindfulness-based intervention training had thicker grey matter (cortical thickness) in their brains, which helps ward off age-related cognitive and mental health diseases, as well as shrinks parts of the brain associated with stress.[124] This is perhaps the most compelling evidence I've seen for the benefits of mindfulness meditation.

Tame Those Tigers

Think back to Lesson 4, in which we explored the concept of negativity bias. Our brains evolved to perceive danger everywhere, yet in reality there is only about one tiger for every 99 we perceive in our minds. The repeated stress responses triggered by those 99 imaginary tigers is detrimental to our overall health. Research has shown that a distracted state of mind is often more anxious, depressed or stressed—any of which can lead to decreased engagement and performance.

The practice of mindfulness can help regulate your limbic system's emotional responses to all those imaginary tigers. It can also help you change your focus away from ruminating on the past, prevent your brain from fretting over disaster scenarios that "would" or "could" happen and bring you back to focusing on your current experience. In short, it helps focus your attention and experience life as it is happening.

Strengthening the Mental Muscle

Attention is a mental muscle; like any other muscle, it can be strengthened through the right kind of exercise. Mindfulness, which is the fundamental exercise for building deliberate attention, is actually quite simple: whenever your mind wanders, notice that it has wandered, bring it back to your desired point of focus and keep it there for as long as you can.

Recently I have been using a phone app to practise Kirtan Kriya meditation. This ancient meditation technique is part of Kundalini Yoga, which has proven to have positive impacts on the brain. Kirtan Kriya combines focused breath with chanting the mantra, "Sa Ta Na Ma." The meditation calls for some portions of the chant to be said out loud, some as a whisper, and some silently. Included as well are finger movements known as mundras, in which you touch each finger to your thumb in sequence while repeating the chant. The best part? The sequence takes only 12 minutes! Admittedly, the whole concept seemed strange, uncomfortable and foreign to me, but the research shared in the Journal of Alzheimer's Disease about the many cognitive benefits of Kirtan Kriya meditation gave me the motivation to give it try. Even within the busy life I lead, I've been able to find 12 minutes a day for this practice. If you're interested in more information, use Google to find videos, articles and research on this effective mindfulness-training technique.

Another great mobile app that helps you exercise your mental muscle through mindfulness meditation can be downloaded at headspace.com. This is a simple app that I use to support my mindfulness practice. I love the pragmatic approach and voice of founder, Andy Puddicombe, a meditation and mindfulness expert who has done a great job of simplifying mindfulness for beginners and busy people. As a mom and an executive, my phone is almost always with me, but with an app like this, brain training is always with me as well. It's one of the upsides of being tied to a mobile device.

Whether you choose a technological aid like Headspace or you go the old-fashioned way and simply find some quiet time for inward focus, your brain will reward you dearly for paying attention.[125]

Mindful Breathing

Gaining control of my unruly mind has been a journey. The best practice that I've discovered is to focus on my breathing. This simple strategy is one of the most efficient ways to learn to focus your mind, because your breathing is with you all the time and you can do it anywhere.

The average person breathes about 23,000 times every 24 hours—it's something we do without even thinking about it. In the words of Dr. Andrew Weil, a pioneer and leader in the field of integrative medicine and holistic health, "Practicing regular, mindful breathing can be calming and energizing and can even help with stress-related health problems ranging from panic attacks to digestive disorders."[126]

Here are two mindful-breathing exercises, developed by Dr. Weil:

4-7-8 Relaxing Breath Exercise

A calming technique for the nervous system, best performed in a seated position. Place the tip of your tongue on the roof of your mouth behind your front teeth, and keep it there for the exercise:

- ▶ Exhale fully through your mouth, making a whooshing sound.
- ▶ Close your mouth then inhale through your nose to a mental count of four (4).
- ▶ Hold that breath for a count of seven (7).
- ▶ Exhale through your mouth with a whoosh sound for a count of eight (8).

That's considered one cycle. The cycle should be repeated three more times; don't exceed more than four cycles during your first month of practice. This exercise is beneficial for decreasing stress and reducing tension, and it is also helpful for falling asleep.

Breath Counting

This breathing technique is a form of meditation often used in Zen practice.

Begin by sitting in a comfortable position with your spine straight and head slightly inclined forward. Close your eyes and take a few deep breaths. Then let the breath come naturally without trying to influence it. Depth and rhythm may vary but should be slow and quiet.

To begin the exercise, count "one" to yourself as you exhale.

The next time you exhale, count "two," and so on, until you reach "five" (to be clear, you're just counting your exhalations, not holding them for that count).

Then begin a new cycle, counting "one" on the next exhalation.

Count only when you exhale, and don't be surprised if your attention wanders. Start with trying five minutes of meditation and work up to ten minutes, and so on.

Each of these exercises can be done anywhere, takes little time and requires no equipment. Like any new exercise regime, learning to breathe mindfully takes practise and commitment, but you'll quickly find the benefits are worth it!

There are many resources available to help you train your brain to focus. Try some and figure out which ones will work best for you and your schedule.

You've got this; you can pay attention. Just like your mother told you to.

NOTES FOR PART V

I want to remember:

_____

I want to stop:

_____

I want to start:

_____

The biggest thing preventing me from taking action is:

_____

I plan to overcome this by:

_____

Two things I will do are:

1. _____

2. _____

The day I will start is:

_____

PART VI

CHANGE

Merriam-Webster's definition of "change" is simply "to make different." We all know, however, that although this can be simply stated, it's not always that easy to accomplish. Niccolo Machiavelli recognized this over 500 years ago when he said, "There is nothing more difficult to carry out, nor more doubtful of success, nor more dangerous to handle, than to initiate a new order of things." We may think that things are different in today's day and age, but are they really? In today's business world, more than 70% of all change efforts fail, and inability to lead change is the number one reason why leaders get fired.[127]

Why is this so? Quite simply, because of human resistance to change. Changing the way we think or behave takes focused attention and considerable brain energy, which is easily forgone for routine and what is known. The good news is that neuroscience has proven that the old saying, "You can't teach an old dog new tricks," simply isn't true.

Like it or not, change is inevitable. Today's leaders must be able to adapt in order to both change themselves and support others to change.

Leading change, however, is incredibly hard work; if you've ever been part of leading change within an organization you know just how true that is. There are days when giving up seems a lot easier than persevering, and others when it feels like the two steps ahead that were made the day before are erased by three giant steps backward.

As I often say, "Leadership isn't for the faint of heart." At times, it can feel absolutely life-draining. Through my studies of the brain and neuroscience, I've learned that it is our brain that gets in the way of our good intentions to change. Most importantly, I've learned how to help myself and others overcome these obstacles.

Learning something new requires us to consciously think about what we're doing and use the thinking part of the brain. Unfortunately, when the brain is required to learn something new, that challenge is often perceived as a threat, which initiates a fight-or-flight response. The brain's fight response to change could take the form of complaining, stalling or even sabotage. Its flight response could show up as ignoring the need for change or simply giving up.

When leading change, you may find you have naysayers undermining your leadership at every corner. Unfortunately, this is a reality of leadership positions, and something I've also experienced throughout my own leadership journey. There have been those who have intentionally tried to chip away at my credibility when leading change, those who have resisted change so adversely that they eventually decided to (or were told to) move on from the organization and many who just quietly ignored any request to change, hoping that it would go away. Fight or flight.

Do leaders change culture? Or does culture change leaders? In my experience, a culture often changes a leader, and not always for the better. Leaders generally start out with the best intentions of leading change for the greater good, only to hit the wall of those resisting or outright sabotaging the change process. Eventually, many leaders compromise their vision and passion and settle for mediocrity to appease the resisters. Fortunately, the reverse is also true: leaders can influence culture in a positive way, but it takes resilience, patience and consistency. Leaders who change culture for the better are the best kind. They understand how to lead with the brain in mind, and they drive engagement and performance. These are the kind of people we want to work for and with.

Another big reason why change often fails is that leaders fail to consider the social and emotional needs of those impacted by the change. As we learned in Lesson 4, humans have a need for clarity, to feel secure, to feel things are fair, to feel in control and to feel accepted. If any of these things are brought into question because of a change, the amygdala will detect a threat and react. If you keep in mind these kinds of potential threat responses, you can plan accordingly and address issues as they arise.

Unwritten Rules

One of the biggest obstacles to personal and organizational change is unwritten rules. Unwritten rules are things that may not technically be allowed, but we know we can get away with them. Our brains are meant to be efficient; if we know we can get away with something rather than applying extra effort and thinking, we will. Our mothers would have referred to this as being lazy or taking the easy way.

Posted speed limits are a great example of unwritten rules. The posted speed limit might be 50 kilometres per hour, for example, but how fast can you really go? It depends on the unwritten rule in your area. Where speed limits are strictly enforced, those in the area know that the stated speed is the acceptable speed and anything over it will be met with a fine. On the other hand, it might be common knowledge that you can get away with going 10 kilometres per hour over the posted speed limit before you risk getting pulled over. It all depends on the unwritten rule.

When approaching personal or organizational change, it's important that you consider any unwritten rules that may be in play. For example, is it okay to be a few minutes late for meetings? Is it okay to check your phone messages during meetings? Do employees really need to meet their targets, or can they get away with not meeting them? These are all examples of cases where unwritten rules might be working against the culture or change you are trying to achieve. If you can identify the unwritten rules, lead by example, and hold others accountable for the standards that are acceptable, you will make traction toward the desired change.

Renowned management consultant Peter Drucker has been credited with the now-famous quote, "Culture eats strategy for breakfast." A culture will wait until it knows if there are real rewards or punishments associated with the requested change before it will have the motivation to invest the energy required to adopt a new way of thinking or behaving. If the unwritten rule states that we don't really have to change, we won't. The same applies for personal change—if we can continue to get away with our old ways and not be held accountable for adopting a new behaviour, we will very likely carry on with our old habits, old beliefs and old behaviours.

Unless people within your organizational culture accept and buy into the change, it's just a matter of time before it gets rejected. By optimizing the conditions for those you lead for readiness for change, you will be infinitely more successful as a leader.

What I've learned through my experience leading change is that, at the very core, most people aren't opposed to what is being proposed; most are opposed to the brain energy it takes to learn something new. They simply don't want to invest the brain energy needed to change their habits. With perseverance and an understanding of how the brain works in response to change, you can change your organizational culture for the better.

In fact, with your new understanding of threat responses, negativity bias, and the brain's natural resistance to learning new things, you already have a huge advantage.

13

CHANGE YOUR
ATTITUDE

Have you ever been part of a group project that lacked an official leader or had too many people trying to lead? I find these situations really challenging. I'm happy to lead, and I'm happy to follow, but going in circles with nobody taking charge or being allowed to lead without being derailed has caused me a near or full amygdala hijack on a few occasions.

During one of the residencies for my master's program, I was part of a group working late one night to get our project complete and ready for presentation. At one point I felt like I had a great idea so I got up and wrote my thoughts on the whiteboard. It felt good to contribute something for consideration that might work. I sat back down awaiting some discussion. The fellow beside me stood up and wiped everything that I had written on the whiteboard off and proceeded to write his own thoughts down. I was really surprised that my ideas were so quickly disregarded and felt consequently quite hurt. I did what every national and international young leader would do within her leadership master's residency—I sat and sulked for the next hour and didn't contribute anything further! I'm not sure that anyone noticed that I mentally withdrew from the conversation. I know; I'm not proud of that hour. It wasn't very mature or leader-like, but it did serve as a significant learning experience.

Because it was a leadership program, we were required to read and journal. That night, I came across a quote that said, "We judge ourselves by our intentions, and others by their actions." I thought about the quote for a minute in the context of what had happened. I thought my intentions were really good, and his actions were really bad. I felt some validation for my feelings and action. Then I back-tested my theory. I thought, what were his intentions? And it struck me quite profoundly that his intentions were the same as mine—to help the group move forward. Yes, his action was not the best, but once I saw his action through the lens of his intentions, my bad attitude dissipated. I decided that I would share with him my experience and hope that it was something that we could both learn from. And it was. Since that learning, I've used this technique many times.

It wasn't until years later when I learned about the brain that I understood what I had learned was a strategy for managing my emotions and reactions called cognitive reappraisal. When I find myself having a bad attitude, I consider the intentions of the person or people that may have caused me to feel this way. I haven't yet found a case where someone had bad intentions.

Cognitive Reappraisal

When it comes to managing our emotional response to something that has made us feel threatened, or when a change is being forced upon us, a shift in perspective can make all the difference. From a neuroscientific perspective, this is known as cognitive reappraisal, "which is the reframing of an event in our mind in order to change one's emotional response to it."[128] It's not just thinking positively; the strategy is to think about the situation *differently*.

Cognitive reappraisal is about seeing the glass half full rather than half empty. Simply being aware of your emotional state (introspection) and paying close attention to it is enough to change it. How powerful is cognitive reappraisal? Studies have found it to be an effective strategy for managing stress, and it can even be used to lower your heart rate.[129]

In her book, Mindset, Stanford psychology professor Carol Dweck proposes that humans can have a "fixed" or a "growth" mindset.[130] Essentially, a fixed mindset judges everything that happens as good or bad; with a growth mind-set, the mind is open to learning and possibilities. Modeling a growth mindset is essential for leaders, and fostering it in others is necessary for unlocking the willingness to change. Given that neuroscience has proven that we are hard-wired to evaluate and anticipate threats (negativity bias), leaders have their work cut out for them when nurturing a growth mindset.

The coach approach, an "asking" style of leadership (as opposed to a "telling" style), is a great tool for untapping a growth mindset in others. As a leader, rather than telling others what to think, when we ask questions like, "What's possible?" or "How can you think differently about this?" we unleash the growth mindset in those we lead. From experience, I can tell you that this is a powerful strategy for leveraging the growth mindset and engaging others in solutions and action.

In a similar concept to Dweck's fixed vs. growth mindset model, author Marilee Adams introduced the "Learner /Judger" mindset model in her book, *Change Your Questions, Change Your Life.*[131] Adams proposes that understanding the importance of mindsets and questions can have a significant impact on successfully adapting to, facilitating or leading change.

The Judger mindset is reactive, closed, critical and focused on problems and blame. For example, when in the Judger mindset, we might ask questions such as, "Why is this happening to me?" "Why bother?" or "What is their problem?" The Learner mindset, on the other hand, is based on curiosity, open-mindedness, solutions and possibilities. When considering change with a Learner mindset, we might ask questions such as "How can this change benefit me and others?" or "How will this help the team or organization?" The Learner mindset path helps you be thoughtful, strategic, positive and solution-focused.

Because of negativity bias, we must accept our Judger mindset and continually practise a Learner mindset. We all have both mindsets and always will. As Adams points out, if you change your mindset from Judger to Learner, you can change your perspective, your mind and—ultimately—your life.

5 Steps to Change a Bad Attitude

1. **Notice.** Notice that you are feeling negatively. What caused you to feel this way?

2. **Breathe.** Take three deep breaths to calm your mind.

3. **Name it.** As we learned in Lesson 5, naming our emotion helps to calm the emotional mind and engage the thinking mind. Ask yourself, "What emotions am I feeling?"

4. **Change your mindset.** Question intentions and opportunity. Ask yourself, "What was the intention of the person(s) who caused me to feel this way?" and "What's the opportunity here?"

5. **Take care of yourself.** Make sure to be getting quality sleep, physical activity and nutrition when facing change or a difficult situation. This will give you more brain energy to tackle it.

Here's an example: let's say you get to work and you are told that the way you store documents has changed and you will no longer be able to do it the way you used to. (1) Notice your attitude change. (2) Take a few deep breaths. (3) Ask yourself what emotions you are feeling. (4) Ask yourself these questions: Is this really important? How can I think differently about this? What can I learn? What are the benefits? (5) Engage in self-care if needed. These five steps are much more effective than digging in your heels and resisting the change.

Once again, your mother was right. Sometimes all you really need to do is "Change your attitude!"

14

YOU CAN DO ANYTHING YOU PUT YOUR MIND TO

For the last few years, I have been working to build coaching skills with the leaders in our organization. In the beginning, nobody really knew what coaching was or how it pertained to leading others. With a lot of hard work by all, we've been able to grow our coaching competencies and see a shift in our leadership style from "telling" to "asking." Essentially, we're trying to shift from being problem-solvers to facilitators of problem-solving. Every time our focus on improving our individual and collective coaching skills slips from the top of our priority list, we leaders fall back into our old habit of telling others what to do more often than asking them what they think they should or could do. Old habits are hard to break.

Fortunately, the leadership team believes in the value of the coach approach, and each year we make incremental progress to becoming a culture that asks vs. a culture that tells. There is evidence that our efforts have been worth it. Organizational engagement scores continue to be above average, and specifically the scores pertaining to leadership and coaching continue to increase. The success we've achieved has come as a result of our disciplined approach to cultural change. We've put our minds to the task.

The Conscious Competence Learning Model

As our mothers told us, we can do anything we put our minds to. In exploring this lesson, I'd like to introduce two models that outline steps required to carve out new neuropathways in the brain and achieve sustainable change. These models are not at odds with each other; rather, they highlight different aspects of the journey toward change. Once you understand the first, you can begin to apply the second. The first model we'll look at has been incredibly useful to me at times when I've considered change for myself or for others. It has stuck with me for years; perhaps it will stick with you and prove equally useful in your own journey toward change.

With every habit you've embedded in your life, starting from when you were just a baby, you have gone from a place of not knowing something, to learning that something, to having it become so routine that it becomes embedded as a habit. Though this may seem glaringly obvious and straightforward, it's actually a complex process that requires considerable brain energy.

The Conscious Competence Learning Model outlines four stages of learning something new and progressing from a place of incompetence to a place of competence. First proposed in the 1970s[132] and just as relevant today, the Conscious Competence Learning Model is simple, yet it explains the challenging and complex process that underlies the formation of any new habit.

Here is a summary of the four stages:

Stage 1: Unconsciously Incompetent – We don't know what we don't know. The saying "ignorance is bliss" is a good sentiment for this stage. For example, there was a time when we didn't know that not wearing a seatbelt in a car increased our chance of death or injury in an accident. We were unconsciously incompetent—we didn't even know there was a problem so we didn't know we were incompetent.

Stage 2: Consciously Incompetent – In this stage, we know something needs to change, but we haven't changed yet. Perhaps someone comes along and wakes us from our ignorance and advises us that seatbelts save lives. We become conscious of the safety issue but we're not used to wearing a seatbelt, so we continue to forget to put it on. When we notice our forgetfulness, and recall the associated risk, we are conscious of our own incompetence.

Stage 3: Consciously Competent – After more thought, and perhaps some peer pressure or introduction and enforcement of a seatbelt law, we decide that we really want to remember to wear our seatbelt. Now we apply focus in order to achieve the change we want to see, and we begin to carve new neuropathways. This stage requires significant brain energy because we have to use the thinking part of our brain to come up with a new way of thinking or doing things (remember what our mothers said about changing our attitude). In our example, this is the point where we would have to consciously think about putting on our seatbelt. Because this stage requires much more energy than is routine, this is the stage at which people (and organizations) often give up.

Stage 4: Unconsciously Competent – Eventually, with focus and practise, we get to a place where we don't have to think about what we are trying to achieve—it has finally become a habit. Those who persevered through the challenging process of learning, and who can now make the new choice without thinking about it, are unconsciously competent. Hopping in the car and putting on our seatbelt is automatic and takes no effort to remember.

I can't stress enough that moving from a state of mind in which we are "unconsciously incompetent" to one in which we are "unconsciously competent" takes focus and practise. We're not just changing a light bulb—we're rewiring our brain.

How can we use the Conscious Competence Learning Model to support ourselves and others to form new habits and enact lasting change? The second model is based on my personal experience—both as an executive coach and as someone who's led organizational change.

Six Steps for Rewiring the Brain

Whether you want to change something for yourself, or support others to change, try out this successful six-step method that I developed for rewiring the brain:

1. **Care.** For yourself, understand why you care about the change. For those you lead, help your team understand why the change is important for them and the organization. Humans are motivated by extrinsic factors such as rewards and punishments (otherwise known as carrots and sticks), and also by intrinsic factors such as a personal drive to succeed.

2. **Notice**. For yourself, notice the gap between where you are and where you would like to be. For those you lead, help them notice the gap between where they are now and where they would like to be (or need to be), and provide coaching on how to close that gap. Simply ask, "On a scale of 1-10, where are you now in terms of your confidence/competence on the issue at hand?" followed by the question, "On a scale of 1-10, where would you like to be on your confidence/competence on this issue?" This will identify the gap. If there is a small spread, the effort needed for change will be less than if it is a large gap.

3. **Take responsibility**. For yourself, take responsibility for the action needed to change. For your team, establish and communicate responsibility for the action needed for change. Follow up with the question, "On a scale of 1-10, how motivated are you to close the gap between where you are and where you would like to be?" Remember, caring is essential when it comes to motivation. If there is no desire (intrinsic or extrinsic motivation) to change, then personal responsibility to change will be unlikely.

4. **Focus**. Keep the needed change top of mind. Focusing on what you and your team members are trying to achieve causes chemical and physical changes in the brain and starts to create the new neuropathways needed to create new habits. The human brain is malleable and changes with experience (neuroplasticity). You can reorganize and restructure your brain, and you can support this restructuring for your team, simply by paying attention to what you all think about. As we've learned, paying attention takes brain energy. Account for extra energy you and others will need to focus on the change at hand.

5. **Be aware of expectations**. If you think you can you will, if you think you can't you won't. Research has shown that what we expect a situation to be like (positive or negative) plays a huge role in what we focus on, what we hear and, ultimately, what transpires. For example, students who are told that they are smart will do better on a test than those students who are told they aren't smart.

This concept isn't new to us. We learned it a long time ago when our mothers read to us from *The Little Engine that Could* and we heard those words, "I think I can. I think I can. I think I can." This concept is known as self-efficacy; believing you can succeed impacts your ability to succeed.[133]

The concept of *what we expect is what we experience* can also be known as the placebo effect, which you may recognize more in terms of medicine. Once thought to be a nuisance in research, the placebo effect is now a crucial part of our understanding of the brain's potential. The placebo effect has taught us that if we believe in something (for example, the effect of a pill for medical improvement), our minds have the power to make it so. As you navigate your way through change, manage your internal commentator to focus on what "will be" rather than what "could be" or "couldn't be." The placebo effect is real, and it can play a key role in reshaping the brain.

Unfortunately, the opposite can also be true, and this is known as the Golem Effect. The Golem Effect occurs when someone has lower expectations of another person, and again this becomes a self-fulfilling prophecy but in a negative way as lower performance is achieved.[134] This effect has significant organizational implications and is a result of poor leadership. The art of leadership is having high enough expectations of others that stretch them to their potential, while not causing undue stress from unrealistic expectations (essentially finding the optimal arousal point for those you lead as noted in the Goldilocks Principle in Lesson 10).

6.   **Practise**. Practise the new way of thinking yourself. For those you lead, allow time to practise the new way of thinking. A study by Phillippa Lally reported that it takes, on average, 66 days to change a habit.[135] Logic would suggest that how long a habit takes to change depends on how deeply embedded the habit is, and Lally's research backs that up. Though 66 days was the average, the actual time required for change in her study ranged from 18 days to 254 days.

The amount of focus and practise that you'll need to apply to you or your organization's own change initiative will likewise depend on how deeply ingrained the habit or "old way" is. Because this focus and practise requires brain energy, self-care is another critical component of achieving sustainable change. Sleep, activity, nutrition and stress management (for you and those you lead) will all play into your ability to focus and practise your new way of thinking or doing.

Try this activity:

1. Get a piece of paper and a pen or pencil.

2. Write your name in cursive on the paper. Approximately how much time did it take you to write your name?

3. Now write your name using the opposite hand. How much time did it take you?

4. Try writing your name with your non-dominant hand three more times. Are you getting a little bit faster?

As you likely experienced, when you attempt to change something that your brain considers routine:

— it generally takes longer (INCREASED TIME).

— you need to use more brain energy (INCREASED THINKING).

— the quality is usually compromised (DECREASED QUALITY).

What was the result of practising writing your signature with your non-dominant hand three more times? You likely found that:

— the time it took started to decrease (DECREASED TIME).

— by the third time, your brain had to work a little less hard to complete the task (DECREASED THINKING).

— the quality started to improve (INCREASED QUALITY).

This simple exercise provides clear evidence that changing a habit is hard work for the brain. It also shows that with focus and practise, the brain can adapt and make room for new ways of doing things. That's neuroplasticity.

Or, as our mothers said, "Practise makes perfect."

Change isn't easy. A lot can get in the way of willingness to change—from attitudes, beliefs and social threats to unwritten rules, exhausted brains and physical factors like lack of sleep, exercise and nutrition. With a better understanding of how your brain and the brains of those you lead process change and, more importantly, the steps required to rewire your brain, you are now ready to lead sustainable change, be it for yourself or for your organization.

As unlikely as it may have sounded at the time, it appears that once again Mom was right—you really can do anything you put your mind to.

15

ALWAYS WEAR CLEAN
UNDERWEAR

Did this lesson get your attention? If so, great! This gem from my mom was included to do just that. As discussed in Part V, in a world of distractions, getting anyone's attention is really hard to do.

Wisdom from mothers and neuroscientists is woven through all of the lessons in this book, but I often wondered what my mom was talking about with this one. Was she really concerned about the kind of impression I would make if I were to be rushed to the hospital in a life-threatening situation? No, probably not. I think Mom's advice in this area was more about planning for unforeseen circumstances, which in a large part describes the way that I have navigated my life and career.

I like to be prepared for change and whatever is coming at me. I feel best when I am prepared; and when I feel good, my brain feels good—and vice versa. And when I pay close attention to self-care—which also takes preparation and planning—my brain is better supported to make good choices and lead others more effectively. Sorry, Mom, I didn't find a lot of neuroscience to back this one up—but it still seems like good advice, and you can rest assured I am in compliance with this lesson!

If/When-Then Planning

Psychologist Robert Cialdini suggests a strategy, called if/when-then planning, to help us achieve our goals. The method goes along with the first of the six steps to rewiring the brain—to notice. More specifically, the method trains us to prepare to notice cues that we want to act on automatically.

Cialdini compares this brain-training method to the way hyperlinking works on a computer. "These goals exist as prefetched sources of information and direction that have been placed on standby, waiting to be launched into operation by cues that remind us of them," he writes in his book, *Pre-Suasion.*[136] This strategy helps us to be more *prepared* for the change that we are trying to implement.

Let's say you want to start taking the stairs up to your office rather than the elevator. You can train your brain by working through an if/when-then plan before your next trip to the office. Your plan might be something like *if/when* I see the elevator door, *then* I will choose to take the stairs instead. You train your brain to associate a specific cue—like the elevator door—with the desired action. Seeing the door reminds you to take the stairs.

Here's where Mom's wisdom comes in about preparing for unforeseen circumstances. Leverage your negativity bias to help plan for things that could go wrong. In this example, you might absent-mindedly walk on to the elevator with a throng of coworkers in a scenario where someone else had pressed the button. Therefore, you need to prepare a better plan. Is there another cue that could trigger your if/when-then plan in advance of standing outside an open elevator door resisting the urge or habit to get on?

Our mothers already understood this strategy of preparing for the worst, and they impressed it upon us with advice such as "Bring a change of clothes," or "Always wear clean underwear."

NOTES FOR PART VI

I want to remember:

_____

I want to stop:

_____

I want to start:

_____

The biggest thing preventing me from taking action is:

_____

I plan to overcome this by:

_____

Two things I will do are:

1. _____

2. _____

The day I will start is:

_____

CONCLUSION

The epidemic of employee disengagement is a problem in most workplaces, and there are physical and financial costs for employees and their organizations. Engagement drives performance, performance drives revenue, and revenue drives growth and sustainability. Engagement is directly related to the bottom line. To increase employee engagement, we need to change the way we lead.

Great leaders set the conditions for teamwork and collaboration. They tap into and utilize the basic lessons they've learned to effectively lead themselves and others. The 15 lessons in this book are relevant and valuable to our leadership journey whether we learned them from our mother, father, teacher, pastor, employer, a book or television. They are the common wisdoms of our societies. As our mothers would say, "You know this stuff."

If we know the lessons, then why haven't we been applying them? Is there something that holds us back from listening to our mothers? Is it our instinctual drive to become independent? My older son, Austin, has come to realize that the lessons I shared with him growing up play an important part in his well-being, but my younger son, Carter, isn't yet convinced. He was seven years old when I told him the name of this book, and he said, "That's not a good idea, Mom. You're only right about 20 per cent of the time."

We all have to find our own way, and I know that my mother wasn't *always* right about what's been best for me. But when it comes to these basic truths that support our ability to think effectively and lead ourselves and others, she was definitely right. Although sometimes ignoring Mom's advice might be the right approach, the neuroscience presented in this book validates the lessons that our mothers shared with us as we grew up—on how to take care of our brains to lead more effectively.

Here's a quick recap of the book. Start with the basics—sleep, activity and nutrition—so that your brain has the best chance at survival in any situation. Understand negativity bias, and manage your own emotions so you can model self-control for others. To ensure effective collaboration, make sure everyone feels accepted and part of the team. Be nice, and keep negativity to yourself so that it doesn't spread to others. Personal and organizational change is possible. It takes plenty of focus, belief that it's possible, preparation, and practise.

When it comes to leadership, the most important thing is to lead by example. Leadership is action, not position, and it starts with you. I'm fortunate that my mom not only passed along her wisdom with each of these unexpected lessons, but she also led by example. My intention is to do the same for my children—and for others whom I have the privilege to lead. Thanks, Mom.

PERSONAL CHANGE PLAN

Are you ready to further leverage these age-old lessons from your mother to support your personal and organizational leadership? Great! To complete an action plan for personal change, use the notes you've made at the end of each section to identify key areas where you would like to see impact. Choose just one or two things that you want to act upon in order to achieve sustainable change.

A. Goal #1:

_____

_____

B. This focus will benefit me and others because:

_____

C. I will know I have been successful when:

_____

D. Barriers - The things that may get in my way are:

_____

I will overcome these by:

_____

E. Strategies for growth will include (consider who, what, when and where):

☐ Coaching/Mentorship

☐ Experience

☐ Reading

☐ Formal Training

☐ Other

F. My Action Plan - 3-5 things I plan to do to achieve my goal are (ensure these 3-5 Actions are SMART: Specific, Measurable, Achievable, Relevant, and Time-bound):

1. _____

2. _____

3. _____

4. _____

5. _____

G. Who can support me and how I will keep this top of mind:

_____

A. Goal #2:

_____

_____

B. This focus will benefit me and others because:

_____

C. I will know I have been successful when:

_____

D. Barriers - The things that may get in my way are:

_____

    I will overcome these by:

_____

E. Strategies for growth will include (consider who, what, when and where):

    ☐ Coaching/Mentorship

    ☐ Experience

    ☐ Reading

☐ Formal Training

☐ Other

F. My Action Plan - 3-5 things I plan to do to achieve my goal are (ensure these 3-5 Actions are SMART: Specific, Measurable, Achievable, Relevant, and Time-bound):

1. _____

2. _____

3. _____

4. _____

5. _____

G. Who can support me and how I will keep this top of mind:

_____

You've got this. As Mom said:

You can do it!

Notes:

_____

_____

_____

_____

_____

_____

_____

_____

_____

_____

_____

_____

_____

_____

_____

_____

CITATIONS

1   The State of the Global Workplace: A worldwide study of employee engagement and wellbeing. (2011). *Gallup.* Pg. 8.

2   Passion At Work: Cultivating Worker Passion As A Cornerstone Of Talent Development. (2014). *Deloitte Center for the Edge.* Deloitte University Press. Web. 10 Dec. 2015.

3   The High Cost of Disengaged Employees. (2002). *Gallup.* Retrieved from http://www.gallup.com/businessjournal/247/high-cost-disengaged-employees.aspx

4   Disengagement Can Be Really Depressing. (2010). *Gallup.* Retrieved from http://www.gallup.com/businessjournal/127100/Disengagement-Really-Depressing.aspx

5   Workplace stress leads to less productive employees. (2016). *Towers Watson.* Retrieved from https://www.towerswatson.com/en/Press/2014/09/Workplace-stress-leads-to-less-productive-employees

6   Hudson, J. (2016). *Compsych.com.* N.p., Web. Jan. 2016.

7   Trends In Global Employee Engagement. (2015). Aon Hewitt.

8   Annual Sleep In America Poll Exploring Connections With Communications Technology Use And Sleep - National Sleep Foundation. (2016). *Sleepfoundation.org.* N.p., Web. Aug. 2016.

9   Pilcher, J.; Huffcutt, A. (1996). *Effects of sleep deprivation on performance: A meta-analysis, Journal of Sleep Research & Sleep Medicine.* Vol 19(4), 318-326.

10 Frenda, S.; Fenn, K. (2016). *Sleep Less, Think Worse: The Effect of Sleep Deprivation on Working Memory.* Journal of Applied Research in Memory and Cognition. Vol 4(4), 463-469, ISSN 2211-3681.

11 Diekelmann, S.; Born, J. (2010). The memory function of sleep. *Nature Reviews Neuroscience,* 114-126 doi:10.1038/nrn2762.

12 National Transportation Safety Board. (1990). *Marine Accident Report: Grounding Of The U.S. Tankship Exxon Valdez On Bligh Reef, Prince William Sound, Near Valdez, Alaska March 24, 1989.* Springfield, VA: National Transportation Safety Board. Print.

13 International Atomic Energy Agency (1986). *Summary Report on the Post-Accident Review Meeting on the Chernobyl Accident, INSAG Series No. 1, IAEA, Vienna.*

14 National Transportation Safety Board. (2001). *Runway Overrun During Landing, American Airlines Flight 1420.* McDonnell Douglas MD-82, N215AA, Little Rock, Arkansas, June 1, 1999. Aircraft Accident Report NTSB/AAR-01/02. Washington, DC.

15 Lack Of Sleep Damages The Brain Like Being Hit On The Head. (2013). Mail Online N.p., Web. 19 Jan. 2016.

16 Ferrara, M et al. (2001). *Sleep Medicine Reviews.* Vol 5(2), 155-79.

17 Neckelmann, D. et al. (2007). *Chronic Insomnia as a Risk Factor for Developing Anxiety and Depression*, Sleep. Vol 30(7), 873-880.

18 Fryer, B. (2006). *Sleep Deficit: The Performance Killer.* Harvard Business Review. N.p., Web. 10 Aug. 2016.

19 Brzezinski, A. (1997), *Melatonin in Humans.* The New England Journal of Medicine. Vol 336,186-195.

20 Wood, B.; Rea, M.; Plitnick, B.; and Figueiro, M. (2013). Light level and duration of exposure determine the impact of self-luminous tablets on melatonin suppression. *Applied Ergonomics.* Vol 44(2), 237-240, ISSN 0003-6870, https://doi.org/10.1016/j.apergo.2012.07.008

21 Mullington, J.; Haack, M.; Toth, M.; Serrador, J.; and Meier-Ewert, H. (2009). Cardiovascular, Inflammatory, and Metabolic Consequences of Sleep Deprivation, *Progress in Cardiovascular Diseases.* Vol 51(4), 294-302, ISSN 0033-0620, http://dx.doi.org/10.1016/j.pcad.2008.10.003

22 Sitting: Your Brain's Mortal Enemy | Extreme Natural Health News. (2017). *Extremenaturalhealth.com.* Retrieved from http://www.extremenaturalhealth.com/sitting-your-brains-mortal-enemy

23 Mercola, J. (2016). Exercise Helps Improve Brain Growth And Regeneration. *Mercola.com.* N.p., Web. Aug. 2016.

24 Ferris, L.; Williams, J.; and Shen, C. (2007). The Effect Of Acute Exercise On Serum Brain-Derived Neurotrophic Factor Levels And Cognitive Function. *Medicine & Science in Sports & Exercise* Vol 39.4, 728-734. Web.

25 Medina, J. (2008). *Brain Rules.* Seattle, WA: Pear Press. Print.

26 Killgore, W.; Olson, E.; Weber, M. (2013). Physical Exercise Habits Correlate With Gray Matter Volume Of The Hippocampus In Healthy Adult Humans. *Sci. Rep.* 3: Web.

27 Mathers, C.D., et al. (2006). *PLoS Med.* Nov 3(11):e442.

28 Van U.; Van G.; Burton, N.W.; Peeters, G.; Heesch, K.C.; and Brown, W.J. (2013). Sitting-time, physical activity, and depressive symptoms in mid-aged women. *American Journal Of Preventive Medicine*, Vol 45(3), 276-281. doi:10.1016/j.amepre.2013.04.009.

29 Exercise, Depression, and the Brain. (2017). Healthline. Retrieved from http://www.healthline.com/health/depression/exercise

30 Exercise as a treatment for depression: A meta-analysis adjusting for publication bias (2016). *Journal of Psychiatric Research.* Jun;77:42-51. doi: 10.1016/j.jpsychires.2016.02.023. Epub 2016 Mar 4.

31 Oppezzo, M.; Schwartz, D. (2014). Give your ideas some legs: The positive effect of walking on creative thinking. *Journal of Experimental Psychology: Learning, Memory, and Cognition*, Vol 40(4), 1142-1152.

32 Godman, H. (2017). *Regular exercise changes the brain to improve memory, thinking skills - Harvard Health Blog.* Harvard Health Blog. Retrieved from http://www.health.harvard.edu/blog/regular-exercise-changes-brain-improve-memory-thinking-skills-201404097110

33 Godman, H. (2017). *Regular exercise changes the brain to improve memory, thinking skills - Harvard Health Blog.* Harvard Health Blog. Retrieved from http://www.health.harvard.edu/blog/regular-exercise-changes-brain-improve-memory-thinking-skills-20140409711

34 Erickson, K.I.; Gildengers, A.G.; and Butters, M. A. (2013). Physical activity and brain plasticity in late adulthood. *Dialogues in Clinical Neuroscience, 15*(1), 99–108.

35 Dementia – Signs, Symptoms, Causes, Tests, Treatment, Care (2017). *Alz.org.* Retrieved Feb 2017 from http://www.alz.org/what-is-dementia.asp

36 Alzheimer's Disease International. (2015). Retrieved from https://www.alz.co.uk/research/WorldAlzheimerReport2015.pdf

37 Chen, W.; Zhang, X.; and Huang, W. (2016). Role of physical exercise in Alzheimer's disease (Review). *Biomedical Reports*, 4, 403-407. https://doi.org/10.3892/br.2016.607

38 Preventing Alzheimer's Disease or Other Dementias: What You Can do to Reduce Your Risk of Alzheimer's Disease. (2017). *Helpguide.org.* Retrieved from https://www.helpguide.org/articles/alzheimers-dementia/alzheimers-and-dementia-prevention.htm

39 What The Outdoors Does To Your Brain. (2017). *Tetongravity.com*. Retrieved from http://www.tetongravity.com/story/culture/what-the-outdoors-does-to-your-brain

40 Gladwell, V.F.; Brown, D.K.; Wood, C.; Sandercock, G.R.; and Barton, J.L. (2013). The great outdoors: how a green exercise environment can benefit all. *Extreme Physiology & Medicine*. Vol 2(3). doi:10.1186/2046-7648-2-3.

41 Poor Workplace Nutrition Hits Workers' Health And Productivity, Says New ILO Report. (2005). *Ilo.org*. N.p., http://www.ilo.org/global/about-the ilo/newsroom/news/WCMS_005175/lang--en/index.htm

42 Healthways, Inc.: Poor Employee Health Habits Drive Lost Productivity According To Major New Study Of Nearly 20,000 American Workers | 4-Traders. (2016). *4-traders.com*. N.p., Web. Jan. 2016.

43 Nutrition And Brain Health | Myvmc. (2010). *myVMC*. N.p., Web. Aug. 2016.

44 Can a Poor Diet Lead to Brain Shrinkage? (2017). *Medscape*. Retrieved from http://www.medscape.org/viewarticle/851596

45 WHO | Micronutrient Deficiencies. (2017). *Who.int*. N.p., Web. 4 June 2017.

46 Moffatt, E et al. (2011). The Cost Of Obesity And Overweight In 2005: A Case Study Of Alberta, Canada, *Canadian Journal of Public Health* 102.2, 144-148. Print.

47 Overweight and obese adults (2014). *Statcan.gc.ca*. Retrieved from http://www.statcan.gc.ca/pub/82-625-x/2015001/article/14185-eng.htm

48 Akbaraly, T.N.; Brunner, E.J.; Ferrie, J.E.; Marmot, M.G.; Kivimaki, M.; and Singh-Manoux, A. (2009). Dietary pattern and depressive symptoms in middle age. *The British Journal of Psychiatry*, 195(5), 408–413. http://doi.org/10.1192/bjp.bp.108.058925.

49 Zellner, D.A.; Loaiza, S.; Gonzalez, Z.; Pita, J.; Morales, J.; Pecora, D.; and Wolf, A. (2006). Food selection changes under stress, *Physiology & Behavior*, Vol 87(4), 789-793, ISSN 0031-9384, http://dx.doi.org/10.1016/j.physbeh.2006.01.014

50 Publications, H. (2017). *Why stress causes people to overeat - Harvard Health. Harvard Health*. Retrieved from http://www.health.harvard.edu/newsletter_article/why-stress-causes-people-to-overeat

51 MD, E. (2017). Nutritional psychiatry: Your brain on food - Harvard Health Blog. *Harvard Health Blog*. Retrieved from http://www.health.harvard.edu/blog/nutritional-psychiatry-your-brain-on-food-201511168626

52 University of California - Los Angeles. (2008). Scientists Learn How Food Affects The Brain: Omega 3 Especially Important. *ScienceDaily*. Retrieved from www.sciencedaily.com/releases/2008/07/080709161922.htm

53 MD, E. (2017). Nutritional Psychiatry: Your Brain On Food - Harvard Health Blog. *Harvard Health Blog*. N.p., Web. May 2017.

54 Neimark, N. (2016). The Fight Or Flight Response - 5 Minute Stress Mastery. *Thebodysoulconnection.com*. N.p., Web. May 2016.

55 Ito, T.A.; Larsen, J.T.; Smith, N.K.; and Cacioppo, J.T. (1998). *Journal of Personality and Social Psychology*, Vol 75(4), 887-900. http://dx.doi.org/10.1037/0022-3514.75.4.887

56 Baumeister, R.F.; Bratslavsky, E.; Finkenauer, C.; and Vohs, K.D. (2001). Bad is stronger than good. *Review of General Psychology*. 5:23-370.

57 Baumeister, R.F.; Bratslavsky, E.; Finkenauer, C.; and Vohs, K.D. (2001). Bad is stronger than good. *Review of General Psychology*. 5:23-370.

58 Hargrove, R.A. (2008). *Masterful Coaching*. 1st ed. San Francisco, Calif: Jossey-Bass. Print.

59 About - Dr. David Rock. (2017). Dr. David Rock. N.p., Web. 4 June 2017.

60 Rock, D.; Cox, C. (2012). *SCARF® in 2012: updating the social neuroscience of collaborating with others* (4th ed.). Neuroleadership Institute.

61 Achor, S. (2011). *The happiness advantage* (1st ed.). London: Virgin.

62 Lieberman, M.D. (2009). The Brain's Braking System (And How To 'Use Your Words' To Tap Into It). *NeuroLeadership Journal* 2 n. pg. Web.

63 Lieberman, M.D. (2009). "The Brain's Braking System (And How To 'Use Your Words' To Tap Into It)". *NeuroLeadership Journal* 2: n. pg. Web.

64 Goleman, D. (1995). *Emotional Intelligence: Why It Can Matter More Than IQ*. New York: Bantam Books. Print.

65 Palmer, S. (2015). Mind the Gap. *Stephen Palmer*. N.p. Web. 4 July 2016.

66 Logan, D; King, J; and Fischer-Wright, H. (2014). *Tribal Leadership*. 1st ed. HarperCollins e-Books. Print.

67 For Love or Money: A Common Neural Currency for Social and Monetary Reward. (2008). *Neuron*, Vol 58(2), 24,164-165.

68 Sherif, M.; Harvey, O.J.; White, B.J.; Hood, W.R.; and Sherif, C.W. (1961). *Intergroup conflict and cooperation: The Robbers Cave experiment (Vol. 10).* Norman, OK: University Book Exchange.

69 McLeod, S. A. (2008). *Robbers Cave.* Retrieved from www.simplypsychology.org/robbers-cave.html

70 Rock, D.; Cox, C. (2012). SCARF in 2012: updating the social neuroscience of collaborating with others, *Neuroleadership Journal 4,* 1-14. Retrieved from http://www.neuroleadership.org

71 Rock, D. (2009). *Your brain at work.* New York: Collins.

72 Meyer-Lindenberg, A.; Domes, G.; Kirsch, P.; and Heinrichs, M. (2011). Oxytocin and vasopressin in the human brain: Social neuropeptides for translational medicine. *Nat Rev Neurosci,* 12 (9), 524–538.

73 Walton, G.M.; Cohen, G.L.; Cwir, D.; and Spencer, S.J. (2012). Mere belonging: The power of social connections. *Journal of Personality and Social Psychology,* 102(3), 513–532.

74 Shirom, A.; Toker, S.; Alkaly, Y.; Jacobson, O.; & Balicer, R. (2011). Work-based predictors of mortality: A 20-year follow-up of healthy employees. *Health Psychol*, 30 (3), 268–275.

75 Holt-Lunstad, J.; Smith, T.B.; & Layton, J.B. (2010). Social relationships and mortality risk: A meta-analytic review. *PLoS Med,* 7 (7), e1000316.

76 Rock, D. (2009). *Your brain at work.* New York: Collins.

77 Slavich, G.M.; Way, B.M.; Eisenberger, N.I.; & Taylor, S.E. (2010). Neural sensitivity to social rejection is associated with inflammatory responses to social stress. *Proc Natl Acad Sci USA,* 107 (33), 14817–14822.

78 Williams, K.D.; Nida, S.A. (2011). Ostracism: Consequences and coping. *Current Directions in Psychological Science,* 20 (2), 71–75.

79 Rosen, C.C.; Koopman, J; Gabriel, A.S.; and Johnson, R.E. (2016). Who Strikes Back? A Daily Investigation of When and Why Incivility Begets Incivility. *Journal of Applied Psychology* DOI: 10.1037/apl0000140.

80 Lieberman, M. (2013). *Social: Why Our Brains Are Wired to Connect.* Crown.

81 Eisenberger, N. (2012). 'The pain of social disconnection: examining the shared neural underpinnings of physical and social pain'. *Nature Reviews Neuroscience,* 1, 421-434.

82 DeWall, C. N.; MacDonald, G.; Webster, G. D.; Masten, C. L.; Baumeister, R. F.; Powell, C.; and Eisenberger, N. I. (2010). Acetaminophen reduces social pain: Behavioral and neural evidence. *Psychological Science,* 21 (7), 931–937.

83 Novembre, G.; Zanon, M.; and Silani, G. (2015). Empathy for social exclusion involves the sensory-discriminative component of pain: a within-subject fMRI study. *Social Cognitive and Affective Neuroscience, 10*(2), 153–164. http://doi.org/10.1093/scan/nsu038

84 Brown, B. (2015). Retrieved from http://brenebrown.com

85 Kok et al., (2013). *Psychological Science* Vol 24(7), 1123-1132, 10.1177/0956797612470827.

86 Zimmerman, A. (2017). 32 Ways To Stimulate Your Vagus Nerve (And All You Need To Know About It) – Selfhacked. *Selfhacked.* N.p. Web. May 2017.

87 Science Reveals a Crucial Difference In Your Brain on Thanksgiving vs. Black Friday. (2017). *Mic.com.* Retrieved from https://mic.com/articles/105126/science-reveals-a-crucial-difference-in-your-brain-on-thanksgiving-vs-black-friday#.lNMi6ejxH

88 McCullough, M.E.; Emmons, R.A.; and Tsang, J. (2002). *Journal of Personality and Social Psychology,* Vol 82(1), 112-127.http://dx.doi.org/10.1037/0022-3514.82.1.112

89 Goleman, D.; Boyatzis, R.; and McKee, A. (2002). *Primal leadership.* Boston, Mass.: Harvard Business School Press.

90 Arnsten, A. F. T. (2009). Stress signalling pathways that impair prefrontal cortex structure and function. *Nature Reviews. Neuroscience, 10*(6), 410–422. http://doi.org/10.1038/nrn2648

91 Positive Intelligence. (2012). *Harvard Business Review.* N.p. Web. 14 Aug. 2016.

92 Goleman, D; Boyatzis, R.E.; and McKee, A. (2002). *Primal Leadership.* Boston, Mass.: Harvard Business School Press. Print.

93 Goleman, D; Boyatzis, R.E.; and McKee, A. (2002) *Primal Leadership.* Boston, Mass.: Harvard Business School Press, 2002. Print.

94 *The Neurochemistry of Positive Conversations.* (2017). *Harvard Business Review.* Retrieved from https://hbr.org/2014/06/the-neurochemistry-of-positive-conversations.

95 Barsade, S.G. (2002). The Ripple Effect: Emotional Contagion And Its Influence On Group Behavior. *Administrative Science Quarterly* 47.4: 644. Web.

96   2016 Global mobile consumer survey: US edition | Deloitte US. (2017). *Deloitte United States*. Retrieved from http://www2.deloitte.com/us/en/pages/technology-media-and-telecommunications/articles/global-mobile-consumer-survey-us-edition.html

97   Optimizing Workflow in the Office (Infographic*). (2017). *Online Course Report*. Retrieved from http://www.onlinecoursereport.com/how-to-achieve-the-ever-elusive-state-of-flow-in-the-workplace

98   Does Mind-Wandering Make You Unhappy? (2017). *Greater Good*. Retrieved from http://greatergood.berkeley.edu/article/item/does_mind_wandering_make_you_unhappy

99   Sinek, S. (2014). *Leaders Eat Last: Why Some Teams Pull Together and Others Don't*. Portfolio/Penguin.

100 Sinek, S. (2014). *Leaders Eat Last: Why Some Teams Pull Together and Others Don't*. Portfolio/Penguin.

101 Medina, J. (2008). *Brain rules* (1st ed.). [Seattle, Wash.]: Pear Press.

102 Limitations of the brain. (2017). YouTube. Retrieved from https://www.youtube.com/watch?v=9BdzhWdVaX0&index=3&list=PL53nCCeNj-RQDhbjE9LjvnFad-wdB5bw7

103 Microsoft Canada. (2015). *Attention Spans*. Web. 13 Jan. 2016.

104 Snyder, B. (2015). Half Of Us Have Quit Our Job Because Of A Bad Boss. *Fortune*. N.p. Web. 10 Dec. 2015.

105 Mindtools.com. (2015). *The Inverted-U Model: Balancing Pressure and Performance*. Retrieved from https://www.mindtools.com/pages/article/inverted-u.htm

106 Szalavitz, M.; Szalavitz, M. (2015). *The Goldilocks Principle of Stress: Too Little Is Almost As Bad as Too Much | TIME.com*. *TIME.com*. Retrieved from http://healthland.time.com/2011/12/20/the-goldilocks-principle-of-stress-too-little-is-almost-as-bad-as-too-much

107 Rock, D. (2013). Why Organizations Fail. *Fortune*. N.p. Web. 14 Aug. 2016.

108 Davis, J. (2005). *Two awesome hours*. New York: Harper One.

109 Hotz, Robert. (2016). A Wandering Mind Heads Straight Toward Insight. *WSJ*. N.p. Web. 14 Aug. 2016.

110 The Science of Making Learning Stick: An Update to the AGES Model. (2014) (1st ed.). Retrieved from http://www.creativedgetraining.co.uk/wp-content/ uploads/2015/07/The-Science-of-Making-Learning-Stick-AGES-Model.pdf

111 10 Great Life Lessons From Albert Einstein. (2016). *Virtuesforlife.com*. N.p. Web. 4 Aug. 2016.

112 Salzberg, S. (2014). Debunking The Myth Of Multitasking. *The Huffington Post*. N.p. Web. Aug. 2016.

113 Loder, V. (2016). Why Multi-Tasking Is Worse Than Marijuana For Your IQ. *Forbes.com*. N.p. Web. Aug. 2016.

114 BBC NEWS | UK | Infomania' Worse Than Marijuana. (2016). *News.bbc.co.uk*. N.p. Web. 3 Aug. 2016.

115 Dmu.ac.uk. (2015). Heavy Internet Users More Likely To Make 'Mistakes' In Daily Life, DMU Research Shows. N.p. Web. 14 Jan. 2016.

116 Salzberg, S. (2013). *Real happiness at work* (1st ed.). New York: Workman Publishing.

117 Mark, Gloria et al. (2016). Neurotics Can't Focus. *Proceedings of the 2016 CHI Conference on Human Factors in Computing Systems - CHI '16*: n. pag. Web. Aug. 2016.

118 Goldhill, O. (2017). Neuroscientists say multitasking literally drains the energy reserves of your brain. *Quartz*. Retrieved from https://qz.com/722661/ neuroscientists-say-multitasking-literally-drains-the-energy-reserves-of-your-brain/

119 Simon, H.A. (n.d.). *BrainyQuote.com*.

120 Miller, E.K. (2000). The prefrontal cortex and cognitive control. *Nat. Rev. Neurosci.* 1, 59–65. doi: 10.1038/35036228.

121 Morris, R.G.M. (1999). D.O. Hebb: The Organization Of Behavior, Wiley: New York; 1949. *Brain Research Bulletin* 50.5-6: 437. Web.

122 Schutte, N. S.; Malouff, J.M. (2011). Emotional intelligence mediates the relationship between mindfulness and subjective well-being, *Personality and Individual Differences,* Vol 50(7), 1116-1119, ISSN 0191-8869, http://dx.doi.org/10.1016/j. paid.2011.01.037

123 Orme-Johnson, D. (1997). *Am J Managed Care* 3:135-44.

124 Hölzel, B.K.; Carmody, J.; Vangel, M.; Congleton, C.; Yerramsetti, S.M.; Gard, T.; and Lazar, S.W. (2011). Mindfulness practice leads to increases in regional brain gray matter density. *Psychiatry Research*, *191*(1), 36–43. http://doi.org/10.1016/j. pscychresns.2010.08.006.

125 Innes, K.E.; Selfe, T.K; Khalsa, D.S.; Kandati, S. (2017). Meditation and Music Improve Memory and Cognitive Function in Adults with Subjective Cognitive Decline: A Pilot Randomized Controlled Trial. *Journal of Alzheimer's Disease*, 1 DOI: 10.3233/JAD-160867.

126 Weil, A. (2017). Three Breathing Exercises and Techniques | Dr. Weil. *DrWeil.com*. Retrieved from https://www.drweil.com/health-wellness/body-mind-spirit/stress-anxiety/breathing-three-exercises

127 Changing change management. (2017). *McKinsey & Company*. Retrieved from http://www.mckinsey.com/global-themes/leadership/changing-change-management

128 Troy, A. S.; Wilhelm, F. H.; Shallcross, A. J.; and Mauss, I. B. (2010). Seeing the Silver Lining: Cognitive Reappraisal Ability Moderates the Relationship Between Stress and Depressive Symptoms. *Emotion (Washington, D.C.)*, *10*(6), 783–795. http://doi.org/10.1037/a0020262

129 Mauss, I.B.; Cook, C.L.; Cheng, J.Y.; and Gross, J.J. (2007). *International Journal of Psychophysiology*. 66(2):116-24. Individual differences in cognitive reappraisal.

130 Dweck, C. (2012). *Mindset* (1st ed.). London: Robinson.

131 Adams, M. (2016). *Change your questions, change your life* (1st ed.). [United States]: Berrett-Koehler Publishers.

132 Learning a New Skill is Easier Said Than Done - Gordon Training International. (2017). *Gordontraining.com*. Retrieved from http://www.gordontraining.com/free-workplace-articles/learning-a-new-skill-is-easier-said-than-done

133 Self-efficacy | Psychology Concepts. (2017). *Psychologyconcepts.com*. Retrieved from http://www.psychologyconcepts.com/self-efficacy

134 Golem Effect | Psychology Concepts. (2017). *Psychologyconcepts.com*. Retrieved from http://www.psychologyconcepts.com/golem-effect

135 Lally, P.; Van Jaarsveld, C.H.M.; Potts, H.W.W.; and Wardle, J. (2010), How are habits formed: Modelling habit formation in the real world. *Eur. J. Soc. Psychol.*, 40: 998–1009. doi:10.1002/ejsp.674.

136 Cialdini, Robert. (2017). *Pre-Suasion*. 1st ed. [S.l.]: Random House Business. Print.

ABOUT THE AUTHOR

Sandra is a sought-after speaker and facilitator on the topic of leadership. She takes complex topics such as leadership, neuroleadership, and mindfulness and explains them in a relatable way that supports leaders to lead with the brain in mind.

With a Master of Arts in leadership, a certified executive coach (PCC) designation, and a certificate in neuroleadership, she has been the driving force behind increased leadership and coaching capacity in her executive role within the credit union system for over 15 years. Early in her career, she received national and international young leader awards.

Sandra is the founder of the eLeadership Academy, an 8-week online masterclass offered internationally to those looking to grow their leadership and coaching knowledge and impact. She delivers high-value, cost-effective leadership development programs that work in today's competitive environment. Sandra advocates that leadership is everyone's responsibility—and that leadership is predicated on action, not position. Find out more at e-LeadershipAcademy.com.

FOLLOW SANDRA AT:

Blog: SandraMcDowell.com/blog

Twitter: @LeadersThinkBig

Web: SandraMcDowell.com